A COLLECTION OF ESSAY ON CHETAN BHAGAT'S NOVELS

DR. R. VADIVELRAJA

Sincerely Dedicated to my Beloved Wife *M.Porkizhi* *and* My beloved Son Master *V.P.GokulAadithya* for their support in my entire successes...

Contents

Preface

Indian writing in English is the bodies of work of writers in India who write in the English language and whose native or co-native language could be tongue one of the numerous languages of India. It is frequently referred to as Indo-Anglian literature, which comes under the broader realm of postcolonial Literature the production from previously colonised countries such as India.

Fiction is an expression of the most intimate awareness of the society in which it is born and in which it evolves around. The Indian novel emerged not simply as a pure literary exercise, but as an artistic response to the socio-political situation existing in the country. The factors that shaped and moulded the growth of the Indian novel arose as much from the political and social problems of a colonized country as from indigenous narrative traditions of ancient culture, since the mid-nineteenth century.

Of all the forms of literature, fiction is the most faithful, convincing and effective vehicle of a nation's ethos. Fiction is the most potent, pliable and popular means of communicating a creative experience, it evokes touching sentiments and profound thought in and around human life. A novelist can portray the life of the nation more authentically, convincingly and artistically than a poet or a dramatist can do.

The novel as a literary phenomenon is new to India. Epics, lyrics, dramas, short stories and fables have their respectable ancestries, going back to several centuries, but it is only during a period of little more than a century that the novel—the long sustained piece of prose fiction—has occurred and taken roots in India.

The development of formal prose began with the Western impact on Indian culture. As a result, Western classics were at the outset translated. A little later, followed works which were either imitations or inspired by Western models. Early Indian writers used English unadulterated by Indian words to convey an experience which was essentially Indian.

Modern Indian fiction in English is exploring several new genres and sub-genres that are considered to be a healthy trend. It is more urban and modern, exploring themes as varied as aspirations of modern youth, their achievements and frustrations, career stories, contemporary social trends, quest for urban roots, living life as a single woman in big cities, exploring sex and alternative sexuality and middle class Indian dreams set in the background of completely different characters and locales.

In the meantime, a new crop of author such as, Chetan Bhagat has arrived on the international scene and their writings are being appreciated around the globe. The corpus of Indian English fiction has been expanding rapidly in the last few years. Chetan Bhagat's novels are a touch ahead from other contemporary novels as they present some insightful pictures of the reality to the readers. They present a smooth reading and keep the interest of the readers till the end. He has captured the attention and imagination of young India thereby presenting the complete package of the life of the Indian youth.

CHAPTER ONE

Indian English

Indian English is the group of English dialects spoken primarily in the Indian subcontinent. As a result of colonial rule under the British Raj until the independence of India in 1947, English is an official language of India and is widely used in both spoken and literary contexts. The rapid growth of India's economy towards the end of the 20th century led to large-scale population migration between regions of the Indian subcontinent and the establishment of English as a lingua franca between those speaking diverse mother tongues. With the exception of the tiny Anglo-Indian community and some families of full Indian ethnicity where English is the primary language spoken in the home, speakers of English in the Indian subcontinent learn it as a first language in English medium schools and as a second language in regional language medium schools. In cities this is typically at English medium schools, but in smaller towns and villages instruction for most subjects is in the local language, with English language taught as a modular subject. Science and technical education is mostly undertaken in English and, as a result, most university graduates in these sectors are fairly proficient in English. Idiomatic forms derived from Indian literary and vernacular language have become assimilated into Indian English in differing ways according to the native language of speakers. Nevertheless, there remains general homogeneity in phonetics, vocabulary, and phraseology between variants of the Indian English dialect. Introduction after Indian Independence in 1947, Hindi was declared the first official language, and attempts were made to declare Hindi the sole national language of India. Due to protests from Tamil Nadu and other non-Hindi-speaking states, it was decided to temporarily retain English for official purposes until at least 1965. By the end of this period, however, opposition from non-Hindi states was still too strong to have Hindi declared the sole language. With this in mind, the English Language Amendment Bill declared English to be an associate language "until such time as all non-Hindi States had agreed to its being dropped." This has never occurred, as English is now considering as all but essential. For instance, it is the only reliable means of day-to-day communication between the central government and the non-Hindi states. The spread of the English language in India has led it to become adapted to suit the local dialects. However, due to the large diversity in Indian languages and cultures, there can be instances where the same English word can mean different things to different people in different parts of India. *Grammar:* The role of English within the complex multilingual society of India is far from straightforward, it is used across the country, by speakers with various degrees of proficiency; the grammar and phraseology may imitate that of the speaker's first language. While Indian speakers of English use idioms peculiar to their homeland, often literal translations of words and phrases from their native languages, this is far less common in proficient speakers, and the grammar itself tends to be quite close to that of Standard British English. *Phonology:* Indian accents vary greatly. Some Indians speak English with an accent very close to a Standard British (Received Pronunciation) accent (though not the same); others lean toward a more 'vernacular', native-tinted, accent for their English speech. *Vowels:* In general, Indian English has fewer peculiarities in its vowel sounds than the consonants, especially as spoken by native speakers of languages like Hindi, the vowel phoneme system having some similarities with that of English, among the distinctive features of the vowel-sounds employed by some Indian English speakers.

Indian English Literature refers to the body of works by authors in India who write in English and whose native or co-native language could be one of the numerous languages of India. It is also associated with the works of members of the Indian diasporas. The tremendously definition of the adjective “Indian” here is hazy. Many of these writers neither live in India, nor are Indian citizens. As a category, this production comes under the broader realm of postcolonial literature – the production from previously colonized countries such as India .Though one can trace such writers in India to a century back, Indian writing in English has come into force only in the last couple of decades or so, as far as literature goes.

CHAPTER TWO

Indian Writing in English

Indian Writing in English has a very recent history, which is one and half century old. Britishers ruled India for 150 years. India and England had dealt with each other in trade, military and political affairs. During this period, England acquired wealth and empire of India. India, in return, got English language and the concept of constitutional Government. From the historical perspective, Indian English Literature has passed through several phases such as Indo-Anglian, Indo-English, Indian Writing in English and recently Indian English literature. In spite of its various cultures, races and religions Indian Writing in English has successfully recaptured and reflected the multi-cultural, multilingual society. As a result, it has aroused a good deal of interest at home and abroad also. The works of various writers get not only a vast category of readers, but also receive a vast critical praise. The term Indian Writing in English is used in a wider sense. This is the body of works by the writers whose mother tongue is one of the languages of multilingual India. According to K. R. S. Iyengar noted there are three types of Indian writers in English, "First, those who have acquired their entire education in English schools and universities. The Second, Indians who have settled abroad, but are constantly in touch with the changing surrounding and traditions of their country of adoption. And finally, Indians who have acquired English as a second language," Consequently, a large number of Indians were greatly moved by the genuine desire to present before the western readers, an authentic picture of India through their writings. Many Indian writers have chosen English as a medium of expression and left a great impact on different forms of literature. For example Toru Dutt, Pandita Ramabai Saraswati, Sri Aurobindo, Jawaharlal Nehru, Sarojini Naidu, Mulk Raj Anand, R. K. Narayan, Raja Rao, Nissim Ezekiel, NayantaraSahgal, Kamala Das,JayantMahapatra, Anita Desai, Bharati Mukherjee, Salman Rushdie, Shashi Deshpande, and some recent Indian writers such as Arundhati Roy, KiranDesai, ArvindAdiga, Chetan Bhagat and many others. They have been using English to represent the Indian culture and spirit etc. In this connection, the remarks of Randolph Quirk and Raja Rao are worth quoting. Quirk rightly remarks that English is not the private property of the Englishmen. Similarly, Raja Rao says in the Preface of his novel Kanthapura: "One has to convey in a language that is not one's own, the spirit that is one's own. "One can notice 'Indianness' in Indian Writing in English. K. R. SrinivasaIyengar has rightly commented in this regard: "What makes Indo-Anglican literature an Indian literature and not just a ramshackle outhouse of English literature is the quality of its 'Indianness' in the choice of its subjects, in the texture of thought and play of sentiment, in the organization of material and in the creative use of language." Whereas Meenakshi Mukherjee observes: "Whatever be the language in which it is written, a novel by an Indian writer demands direct involvement in values and experiences which are valid in the Indian context." Indian Writing in English expresses a shared tradition, cultural experiences and Indian heritage. Early Indian writers have used many Indian words and the experiences throughout their works of art. R. K. Narayan has created *Malgudi* similar to Thomas Hardy's *Wessex* .Nirad C. Chudhary is famous for his The Autobiography of an Unknown Indian (1951). As figured out by Reddy Venkata K. and Reddy Bayapa P. these writers do comment on the social issues like: "superstitions, casteism, poverty, illiteracy and many other social evils that were eating the vitals of Indian society" .6 Salman Rushdie is the most notable among all the Indian writers in English. His *Midnight's Children(*1980) won the Booker Prize in 1981,the well know writer ShashiTharoor for his *The Great Indian Novel (*1989), Bharati Mukherjee author of *Jasmine*(1989) has spent her career on the issues involving immigration and identity. Vikram Seth is known for his novel *A Suitable Boy* (1994). Other remarkable writers include Khushwant Singh, Anita Desai, Shashi Deshpande, Amitav Ghosh, Bharati Kirchner, Arundhati Roy, Kiran Desai, JhumpaLahiri, C. R. Krishnan, VikasSwarup, ArvindAdiga *Chitra Banerjee Divakaruni* and others. Chetan Bhagat is well known for him unique literary creations like *Five Point Someone* (2004) *One Night @ the Call Center* (2005) *The 3 Mistakes of My Life* (2008)*2 States* (2009) *Revolution 2020* (2011) *Half Girlfriend* (2014) *One Indian Girl* (2016) *The Girl in Room 105* (2018) *One Arranged Murder*(2020) and *400 Days* (2021)

Non-fiction *What Young India Wants* (2012) *Making India Awesome* (2015) and *India Positive* (2019).

Indian Writing in English has witnessed few controversies in its evolvement. It has to prove itself on the grounds of superiority and inferiority compared to literature produced in other Indian languages. It has also witnessed accusations of being superficial, imitative, shallow etc. Indian writers in English have also been criticized of being not real socio-cultural ambassadors of India. They have been said to get themselves uprooted from the authentic Indian sense. However, the new generation of Indian writers in English has handled the wide range of themes and the subject matters. Shashi Deshpande, Shobha De, Arundhati Roy, Kiran Desai, ArvindAdiga Chitra Banerjee Divakaruni and Chetan Bhagat have written on variety of themes. For these writers English is a medium of expression of their creative recommend, through which they can reach to the international readers.

Chetan Bhagat is an icon of new India and he has an enduring name in the ground of postmodern fiction. He has opened the floodgates for a new movement of Postmodernism in Indian Writing in English. His name doesn't grace any awards list, but he is familiar to every college student in India. While the global literary dwell on the fiction of India's past, Chetan Bhagat has become

India's well known writer by embracing the present. He manages to retain his sense of humor even though the topics those are actually harsh realities of life. His writing has revolutionized and mirrored the postmodern literature. According to him, the purpose of literature is to showcase the society.

CHAPTER THREE

Life & works of Chetan Bhagat

Chetan Bhagat was born in New Delhi, India, on 22nd April 1974. His father was an Army officer, and his mother was a government employee in the agricultural department. His younger brother Ketan is also a novelist.

He completed his college years at The Army Public School, DhaulaKuan in Delhi. He received his undergraduate degree in mechanical engineering from the Indian Institute of Technology Delhi in 1995 and his MBA degree from the Indian Institute of Management Ahmedabad in 1997. Bhagat recounted in an interview with News laundry that he applied after his studies to the investment banking company Goldman Sachs, where he was finally selected after 27 internal interviews. Bhagat worked for Goldman Sachs in their Hong Kong office as an investment banker for nearly a decade and wrote *Five Point Someone* while in Hong Kong. He then moved to Mumbai to focus full-time on his writing career while working at Deutsche Bank.

Chetan Bhagat is an author columnist, screenwriter, television personality and motivational speaker, known for his Indian-English novels about young urban middle class Indians. Bhagat also writes columns on youth, career development and current affairs for *The Times of India* (in English) and *Dainik Bhaskar* (in Hindi). Bhagat's novels have sold over seven million copies. In 2008, *The New York Times* cited Bhagat as "the biggest selling English language novelist in India's history". Bhagat was included in *Time* magazine's list of World's 100 Most Influential People in 2010.Bhagat's screenwriting has included the dramatis *Kai Po Che!* (2013), *2 States* (2014), the action-superhero movie *Kick* (2015), and *Half Girlfriend* (2017). He won the Film fare Award for Best Screenplay for *Kai Po Che!*at the 59th Film fare Awards on January 2014. He moved to Amazon Publishing on April 27, 2018 from Rupa Publications as per the news resources, and his first novel with Westland is The Girl in Room 105.

Chetan Baghat, a rising star in the contemporary modern Indian literature, is a multitalented personality. He is a novelist, columnist, public speaker and a screenplay writer. His notable works include *Five Point Someone, The 3 Mistakes of My Life* and *2 States etc*. Most of his literary works address the issues related to Indian youth and their aspirations which earned Baghat status of the youth icon.

While working as a banker he had already began to write manuscripts for his first two novels. His debut novel, *Five Point Someone– What not to do at IIT!,* was published in 2004. The story is centered on three mechanical engineering students with five point GP at IIT, where the author himself had once studied. It deals with the unfair grading system adopted by the higher education system which places students into higher and lower level based on their rote-learning skills. The story is narrated from the first person perspective one of the friends in a light-hearted tone. Essentially, the book targets the ineffective and uninspiring teaching methods and evaluation system employed by the internationally recognized institutions. The author points out that such institution merely produce a stock of engineers based on their ability to memorize everything that has been taught rather than encouraging students to tap into their creativity.

Five Point Someone instantly became both literary and commercial success. Baghat reached at the peak of his popularity with his debut that was later turned into a critically commended film titled, *3 Idiots* (2009). It was followed by his second likewise successful novel, *One Night @ the Call Center*. In fact, it was adapted for big-screen as *Hello* and Baghat himself wrote the screenplay. However, the adaptation failed to capture audience's attention and called a flop. In 2008, he enclosure *The 3 Mistakes of My Life,* which is based on the all-time favorite Indian sports, cricket. The novel gathers positive reviews and the film adaptation released in 2013, *Kai Po Che!,* became a hit.

Baghat's fourth novel, *2 States: The Story of My Marriage* is a autobiographical novel that focuses on the prevailing issue of interstate marriage in India. It is based on Bhagat's and his wife's own experience, who like the protagonist of the novel uncompromisingly tried to convince their respective families of different casts to approve of their marriage. The book highlights the conservative mindset shared by several sects in Indian states which prohibit marriage outside their cast. The book and its film adaptation was a major success. Chetan Bhagat wrote two more books; *Revolution 2020* (2011), and *What Young India Wants* (2012) etc. Additionally, he received Society Young Achiever' award, Publisher's Recognition award and Film fare Award for Best Screenplay.Chetan's style of writing is simple, lucid and vivid with graphic descriptions and linear narratives. Most of the protagonists in his novels are named after Lord Krishna such as Shyam, Krishna, Hari, Govind and Madhav.Bhagat is considered a youth icon rather than being just an author. With his vigorous and humorous way of depicting stories, he has encouraged the habit of reading in many young Indians. According to him, novels are perfect devices for both inspiration and entertainment and through which he disseminates his views and opinion about society and youth.

Novels

- Five Point Someone (2004)
- One Night @ the Call Center (2005)
- The 3 Mistakes of My Life (2008)

- 2 States (2009)
- Revolution 2020 (2011)
- Half Girlfriend (2014)
- One Indian Girl (2015)
- The Girl in Room 105 (2018)
- One Arranged Murder (2020)
- *400 Days* (2021)

Non-fiction

- What Young India Wants (2012)
- Making India Awesome (2015)
- India Positive (2019)

Awards and recognition

- Society Young Achiever award in 2004.
- Publisher's Recognition award in 2005·
- Bhagat in *Time* magazine's list of World's 100 Most Influential People 2010·
- Filmfare Award for Best Screenplay 2014: *Kai Po Che*
- CNN-IBN Indian of the Year in Entertainment in 2015

CHAPTER FOUR

Writing style of Chetan Bhagat

Introduction

Chetan Bhagat is an emerging author an Indian English Literature. His arrival in the world of Indian English Fiction coincided with a time when the presence of a vibrant media culture and the growth of a corporate structure in the urban and semi-urban Indian society was effecting changes in the reading tastes, especially for the younger generation whose incorporation into the corporate design were only increasing. He is a far cry from the typical author image that lies in the mind of the common man and is dealing with the harsh realities of life and problems faced by the young generation in his work and also holds a mirror to society and presents the reflection of the society of our own country.

The secret success for Chetan Bhagat is selection of topics which are common. He selects subjects which the readers can associate with his novel with a mix of sentiment, romance, relationship, religions and politics. His strong narration has people relating to situations, incidents and characters in a natural way. His novel talks about dreams and aspirations of all characters and character seemed more real and simple genuine reservations. His narratives often lean towards the dramatic. The dramatic element is prominent, as Bhagat chose to begin his tales with 'prologues' which either contains the dramatic tell- all as in'2 *States-The story of my marriage*' or compose the most dramatic episode of the book as in

'One Night @ the Call Center'. His 'acknowledgements' are no less dramatic, which often betrays his anxious attempt of highlighting his 'product' as a innovative and better brand, such as his claims in the "Acknowledgements" to *'Three Mistakes of my Life'* that he does not "want to be Indian's most admired writer", he "wants to be India's most loved writer", or his providing the readers with a questionnaire in *One Night @ the Call Center.* Again his novels are called "Acts" and his endings "Epilogues". Not only the dramatic, but he plentifully draws his techniques from the cinematic form as well. His narrative a swing naturally back and forth using the 'flash-back' technique and his language is very lucid and easy to understand too that is largely in sync with fast narrative is full of what is called 'chutnified' expressions, inter-language code-switching which is common on the Internet circuit. Besides this deliberate patterning of the narrative and the diction approach towards the issues, he addresses is part of his wonderful arrangement skill. As for the narrative, Bhagat resorts to the thriller and the fantastic form and also his novel deals with a very serious theme in a light way.

Chetan Bhagat is also famous Indian author who penned down novels that hit the market with great success. All of them were bestsellers since their release and have been filmed by famous Bollywood directors. Chetan Bhagat is considered a youth icon rather than as just an author. With his vivid and humorous way of depicting stories, he has inspired reading habits in many young Indians. He is also a good columnist and writes columns for many leading newspapers. According to him, novels are entertainment tools through which he expresses his views and opinion about society and the youth. Development issues and national issues are addressed through columns. Chetan's columns are written in a way that directly points out the issues within nation and in many times it has even activate discussions in the parliament. He is not only a good writer but also a motivational speaker and has given many motivational speeches at many colleges, organizations and companies.

Life and works of Chetan Bhagat

Chetan Bhagat was born in New Delhi in a middle class Punjabi Family on the 22nd of April, 1974. His father was an Army man and his mother, a government employee. The major part of his education was done at Delhi.

He studied in the Army Public School, Dhaula Kuan, and New Delhi during the years 1978 to 199 after which he chose to do Mechanical Engineering at the Indian Institute of Technology (IIT), Delhi. After pursuing engineering he took up a management program offered at the Indian Institute of Management (IIM), Ahmadabad. Being an outstanding student, it was no wonder when he was recognized as the "Best Outgoing Student" of his batch by IIM Ahmadabad. He later got married to Anusha Suryanarayanan in 1998; she was his fellow student at IIM-A. Chetan then went to Hong Kong along with his family and worked as an investment banker with Goldman Sachs.

He worked in Hong Kong for eleven years and then shifted to Mumbai and started writing. It was his passion. He has six novels against his name: Five Point Someone (2004), One Night @ The Call Center (2005), The Three Mistakes Of My Life (2008 , Two States (2009) and Revolution 2020 (2011), What Young India Wants (2012) . Half Girlfriend (2014) Making India Awesome (2015),One Indian Girl (2016), The Girl in Room 105 (2018),India Positive (2019) and One Arranged Marriage Murder(2020).By chance or by choice, titles of all his novels had numbers associated with them. He now leads a happy life with his wife and twin sons Ishaan and Shyam. Chetan loves to live a simple life watching cartoons with his children who wish to become super heroes. He is an NRI and he is a Singapore citizen. He is a health conscious person and practices yoga regularly.

Chetan Bhagat published his first novel Five Point Someone in 2004 and this very first venture took him to the peaks of fame and popularity. The book depicted the story of an IIT student who considers himself to be below average than all the other students in IIT. This book won the Society Young Achiever's Award and

Publisher's Recognition Award. The story was adopted into a film directed by Rajkumar Hirani and starred famous Bollywood stars like Aamir Khan, Madhavan, Sharman Joshi and Kareena Kapoor.

His second book was One Night @ A Call Center and this too was a great success. This book was made into a movie and was named 'Hello' and Chetan himself wrote the script. The movie was noted by the special appearance of Bollywood star Salman Khan and was an average hit. His next novel has cricket as the major theme. It is named Three Mistakes of My Life. His fourth book is named Two States. His fifth novel is Revolution 2020. His sixth novel is What Young India Wants etc. Chetan Bhagat's contribution to the field of entertainment is noticeable. He never confined his literary talents to just writing novels.

A preamble to writing style

Writing style alludes to the way in which a writer composes for her or his readers. A style displays both the essayist's identity and voice, yet it additionally demonstrates how she or he identifies the audience. The decision of a reasonable written work style shapes the general character of the work. This happens through changes in grammatical structure, parsing composition, including lingual authority, and sorting out of thought along with usable systems. Much the same as design, written work can express a particular style. Writing style is much similar to whatever other sort of styles in which it helps us express who are. It is the means by which the writer communicates him or herself through writing. Every individual has their very own design style, whether they intend to or not. The garments and accompaniments that they wear every day can characterize individual style. The same goes for writing style. There are four principle sorts of writing -expository, persuasive, descriptive, and narrative-and each one has a particular style.

Writing style of Chetan Bhagat

Chetan Bhagat does not take to the bombastic style of writing. His language is simple, clear and quite comprehensive even to the new bees of reading. It is for this reason that school and college goers enjoy his novels. Chetan bhagat's basis is the subject or the content of the story and not its language. Even when the language takes priority, it is straight to the heart. Characters tell their story in no complicated language but directly to the eager listener. His language, though very simple, exactly produces the impact that is needed.' "Two States: The Story of my Marriage" tells you quite humorously but very surely that one among the auto-drivers knew only some English words. So Chetan's eloquence of the language, takes his readers on an easy, comfortable but fascinating travel. They never get ebbed because of the language barrier even though they are surprised due to tremble and twists in the story.

Chetan Bhagat's writing style has a tendency to be simple, with linear narratives and vivid storytelling. His protagonists tend to be named after Lord Krishna, like Hari, Shyam, Govind or Krishna etc.All his novels have a number in the title (eg. 'five' in the first, 'one' in the second, 'three' in the third and 'two' in the four.) When asked about this Chetan Bhagat replied 'I'm a banker, I can't get numbers out of my head."

Chetan Bhagat has always attempted to touch upon something new in his writings. His writing has always been close to reality. He has always expressed himself in a way which is understood by all and every generation can connect itself to it. His thoughts are worded in such a skillful way that they are understood by readers immediately.

Chetan Bhagat novels have always presented a true picture of life in India. And, that has been one of the major reasons, why his novels have captured the minds of the younger generation. As per the Time magazine he is one of the "100 most influential people in the world". People across all age groups read his books. However, they are more popular with the younger generations. His books usually deal with the current trends - be it marriage, work, relationships, or any other issue related to youth. Though he has written a handful of books, he has touched upon a variety of subjects from life at call center, secularism, stress in today's education system, inter – community marriages, corruption, life style of present students and many more. Chetan Bhagat started off his literary career while he was still working as a Banker.

Chetan Bhagat sells way more than the likes of Amitav Ghosh, Salman Rushdie and Co. in India English writer. It is not because he writes better English than them, in fact he doesn't but simply due to the fact he gives something to his audience that others don't – connect. All his novels vibrate with the readers to some degree, they can easily relate to the characters, their issues, their dilemmas and their backgrounds. Moreover the fact that he doesn't use complicated words and heavy prose means that his books are light read and can be easily summary and don't have be chewed slowly bite by bite like the ones by 'sophisticated writers'.

However, his ability to do this has unintentionally earned his readers a tag, especially in bigger cities, that of having bad English and being unintelligent. If one goes to a small town or level II & level III cities in India, then having a Chetan Bhagat book in one's hand is a sign of being intellectual and having good taste in reading. However in metros, especially Mumbai, Chennai, and Delhi one shall meet a fair number of people who look down upon his readers, where Bhagat is bashed good and proper as a 'masala' writer. Motivated by Bhagat's success, many Indians are already on their way to becoming e-book self-publishers after being rejected by mainstream publishing houses. They wouldn't have taken such a bold step had Bhagat not showed them that 'common man's language in writing' sells in the country. In response to poor reviews from critics, Bhagat described the books as entertainment, rather than attempts at serious literature. Chetan Bhagat has often said he writes not to be a literary genius but to get people learn English. Not a good idea at all. (Where Chetan's protagonist Madhav aspires to learn English and where the teachers do not any better from the students) would be as good. Chetan claims to use the common man's language.

Some sections of this society apparently find quality in what Chetan Bhagat writes -- the way his characters behave and talk. But it is just not literary. It might be entertaining (entertainment is different things to different people). When it studies literature, they expect to learn something out of it. Bhagat's geniuses give their nothing. They just confirm the stereotype of society struggles to fight against. Chetan Bhagat, hence certainly recognizes the pulse of a large section of the Indian society. But he should not tar the art of literature.

Hope and Trust

Chetan Bhagat's books give readers a feeling of trust and hope. They understand that part of life by virtue of which they fight what they called 'life'. In a general public damaged by collective sentiments there exists an 'Ali' in "*Three Mistakes of my Life*" who says, "It's alright on the off chance that I don't turn into a player, yet it's not alright if I am not an Indian". Regardless of the possibility that all trust is lost God may come bringing in your mobile phone without a system. Furthermore, despite the fact that a study bounced from the ninth floor in a giftedly sad circumstance his companions are there to safeguard him and take him back to the entryways of new trusts, hope and longings. Caught by dishonor on all fronts, a Gopal Mishra of *'Revolution 2020'* raises over all his piffling desire to guarantee that the new sentiments of advancement and improvement blow in his country. He lets all the fortune summative through out of line means go to hellfire just to be known as a decent and respectable man.

Youth Aspect

Youth is the main focus of Chetan Bhagat's novels. The young generation has its dreams sparkled with the glitters of hope as well as battered with the tales of inabilities of achievement and helplessness against the system. Even though the youth force is said to be able to dislocate mountains and block the flow of rivers, it faces its own problems when it fights the age old red tape and a corrupt infra-structure. The victories and defeats of the youth are trademarks of Chetan bhagat's stories. A young reader sails through his novels as if he or she is living and not just reading the novel.

A piercing climax

In all the stories of Chetan bhagat's novels have observed a nail-biting climax. Be it God's call in *'One night @ the Call Centre'* or saving Ali from the jaws of the riot in '*Three Mistakes of my Life*' or Gopal Mishra's sacrifice in the end game of 'Revolution 2020', there is drama, emotion and twist. Climax is the part of the tale which can provide the real thrill and sums up the story. Chetan bhagat has shown the ability to wind up his novels amazingly.

Writing Style and Characters

The post-modern writers like Kiran Desai, Chetan Bhagat and Arvind Adiga have introduced the youth of contemporary period as caught in the connecting meaningless life. The protagonists of their books are enduring on account of modern disordered existence of dissatisfaction, separation, and depression, lack of involvement, rebellion, uncertainty and illogicality. Every one of the protagonists has been completely severed from the otherworldliness and intellectuality in their everyday life.

Chetan Bhagat's style of composing is basic, clear and characteristic with realistic descriptions and direct stories. The majority of the protagonists in his books are named after Lord Krishna, for example, Shyam, Krishna, Hari, Govind and Madhav. Bhagat is viewed as an youth symbol instead of being only a creator. With his lively and diverting method for portraying stories, he has energized the tendency for perusing in numerous youthful Indians. According to him, books are ideal gadgets for both motivation and stimulation and through which he disperses his perspectives and sentiment about society and youth.

All the modern characters of Chetan Bhagat's books like Ryan in *Five Point Someone,* Shyam in *One Night @ The Call Center*, Govind in *Three Mistakes of My Life*, Krish in 2 States, and Gopal and Raghav in *Revolution 2020* are in issue, what to do and what not to do, what is correct and what is not. They all need to carry on with a decent life and doing great in their life.

Chetan Bhagat does not take to the extravagant style of composing. His language is direct, ordinary and totally extensive. This is the reason that school goers appreciate a large portion of his books. Chetan Bhagat's essential part is the issue or the substance of the story and not its tongue. Despite when the tongue takes need, it is directly to the heart. Characters describe their story in no jumbled vernacular yet clearly to the energized gathering of people.

Conclusion

Chetan Bhagat's books are light and breezy and the language is simple. The author uses a lot of can't words that Indians use every day. The narrative of the story stays fresh though, the ending of the story is expected, still find characters rooting for the lead characters to get together at the end. Bhagat is narrative do 'reflect and deals' neither "technically nor thematically" form. His strong narration has people relating to situations, incidents and characters in a natural way. His novel talks about dreams and aspirations of all characters and character seemed more real with simple genuine fears. In his narrative capability he is looked upon as a pioneer of the new form which is perfectly fit to bring about the issues of the multilingual generation. It doesn't matter how good or bad Chetan Bhagat's English language is. He has converted lakhs of non-readers into readers and has inspired thousands to turn into writers. That is no signifying achievement. His writing has got commercial success to him but has also brought joy to the sufficient.

CHAPTER FIVE

Chetan Bhagat as a Modern Signal in Indian Writing in English

Indian Writing in English was sown during the period of the British rule in India. Now the starting point has flourished into an ever green tree, odorous flowers and ripened fruits. The gooey is being tasted not only by the native people, but they are also being enjoyed by the people outside India. It happened only after the constant caring, pruning, watering and nourishing. Gardeners like Tagore, R.K.Narayan, Raja Rao, M.K Anand, Salman Rushdie, Toru Dutt, Sorojini Naidu, Kiran Desai -to name only a few, looked after the tender plant day and night. In modern time, it is guarded and nurtured by a number of writers due to that vision and maturity advertising awards and accolades all over the world. Indian English Novel of the first generation reflects the rising nationalism and has grown with the nation's independence. The novels show concern with national and social problems. The novels of the 1960s have a private tone focusing on an individual's life and are introspective. Novels from 1980 onwards created a division in the history of Indian English novels as they brought in a significant change in the world view, expression and the form. "The birth and the development of the novel in India 'as genre nursed by, ifnot born out of the tension between opposing systems of values in a colonial society, and modified by certain indigenous pressures." (according to view)

The evolution of the novel writing in English, as a form, in India has been aptly described by *Meenakshi Mukherjee* in her above words. The development of novel, like any other literary form in the nation has been greatly influenced by the issues and environs of independent India. Crisis ill Civilization by *Rabindranath Tagore* is a passionate and uncompromising statement of his loss of faith in Western civilization. The composition not only shows his ultimate disillusionment with the British rule in India, it is also a condemnation of the Western civilization. "I had at one time believed that the springs of civilization would issue out of the heart of Europe. But today when I am about to quit the world that faith has gone bankrupt altogether." (Tagore, II) *Rabindranath*, who had started his life as an ardent believer in the benevolence of the European civilization was later disappointed when he came across the disastrous consequences of the English rule is Indian subcontinent. It is with this disappointment the beginning of Modern Indian English Literature is marked, the earliest phase of which is described by *H.M. Williams* as 'Georgian effusions'.

However, over a period of time, those effusions took a back seat with the British denial to grant Indian Independence. Therefore, the new generation that emerged was disillusioned by the West's failure to keep its heady promises. The early novelists of 1930-40's *Mulk Raj Anand, R.K. Narayan* and *Raja Rao* can be compared to the Four Wheels of 18th century English novelists with themes and skills. These three early masters laid the foundation of the modern English novel in India by adapting English Language to the Indian needs by asserting an Indian Identity. This assertion of identity even by adopting English language was "Declaration of Independence from English Literature" *(R.Parthasarthy)*. It was a creative appropriation of English Language. At the same time it rejected the world of the existing British English Literature as well.

*Mulk Raj Anand'*stheCoolie,*The Untouchable and Two Leaves and A Bud*reveal the heroic suffering, the conflict between national and local sensibility, and the human Concerns for the downtrodden under the guise of Moonu,Bakha and Gangu respectively.*Mulk Raj Anand's* novels express nationalism, social concerns and Gandhi an socialism. His novels arc recognized as an instrument to sec the contemporary history of India. His experiments with social realism and enthusiasm of North Indian dialects, laid the foundation for linguistic and cultural representations in future novels. From South India, *Raja Rao* evokes the magnificent mythical imagination of Indian antiquity successfully in the three novels *-Kanthapura, Serpent'" and Rope* and *Shakespeare* and most of short stories he has written. The classic foreword to *Kanthapura* has been recognized as a manifesto for the path *Raja Rao* had opted and preached for Indian Writing in English. *Raja Rao* resolved the dichotomy of foreign (English) language and methods of Indian story telling tradition through a systematic Indianization of English and a spirit of Indian life. He deviated from the traditional structure ofEuropeannovc1 and shaped it on the lines of the epic tradition of India. He complemented *Mulk Raj Anand's* effort of introducing North India to Indian English Novels by bringing in an unusual blend of South Indian -French cultural outlook and realities. *R.K. Narayan* is realistic fiction writer who depicts the comic mode as equivalent to the tragic in his evocation of mediocrity in metaphorical way with *The Guide, Financial Expert, the Waiting for Mahatma* and other series of novels in an imaginary 'Malgudian' touch. He focused on the anxieties; disappointments and struggles of a generation who stood on the threshold of independence, the point where the institutions established during British Raj were still dominating and negotiating their way into independent India. The great trio of *MulkRaj Anand, RajaRao and R.K. Narrayan* had been penning down fiction in English before and after independence. However, writing fiction in English was not explored much by larger groups of authors in India during this period. In fact, for almost two decades after independence the exercise of writing a novel in English was considered against the norms of loyalty for the nation. It took more than ten years for a novel in English to receive SahityaAcademy award. *R.K. Narayan's* Guide heralded the era of acceptance of English novels by Indian authors as an indigenous genre by winning the SahityaAcademy award in 1960. Indian English novel also developed with the general economic growth and prosperity after temporary setbacks of war and loss of great leaders. The sustained structure of the novel form too added to the arduous nature of representing Indian life in English. Moreover the novel being essentially a Western form imposed certain limits and also subsequently modified the Indian experience. Raja Rao pointed out in the prologue of *Kanthapura*.

In spite of diversity in themes and techniques, the novelists during 1950s and 1960s have some common features like the presentation of personal narratives against the background of modern Indian, honesty, the conflict of values between the family and the individual and the awareness of social change. Indian writers in English in this period were concerned about character development, psychological deepness and an effort to negotiate the sense of alienation in the modern world, albeit, the nature of both 'alienation' and 'modernity' were not the same for India as it was the west. The emergence of women novelists was a significant development of these decades. Women writers like *Kamala Markandaya* with *Nectar In A Sieve, Some inner Furry, A Silence of Desire and A handful of Rice; Santh Rama Rao in Remember The House, while Anita Desai with cry, The Peacock and The Voices In The City* have a fine eye for the urban and city life. Other women writers like *Ruth Prawarjabhwala and NayantaraSahgal*came upon the stage and shared the platform enjoyed by the well-known Indian English writers. These women writers of the first generation engaged themselves with the issues of women in conventional marriage systems, human relationships, and contemporary social and political developments from a woman's point of view along with the psychological influences of contemporary world. *Dr. Babhanibhattacharaya and Khuslmant Singh,* in very different ways gives us valuable insight into the pathos of economic poverty. Misdistributions of wealth and human degradation caused by political upheavals. The novels of these years exhibited a command over the form but lacked innovations. As *Shyamala Narayan and Jon Mee* point out, except one or two examples, "None of the books of this period, ... are interested in developing the conflict between tradition and modernity which are a thematic feature of so many of their stories-into any kind of fonnal exploration of indigenous narrative forms".

Nevertheless several major Indian English novels were published during the 1960s. The conspicuous titles produced during this span of twenty years include-*The Serpent and The Rope, The Cat and Shakespeare, The Guide, The Man Eater of Malgudi, Sunlight on A Broken Column Bend in The Ganges, Storm in Chandigarh, A Handful of Rice, Nectar in A Sieve, Bye Bye Black Bird, Cry, The Peacock.* There was no huge spurt of creativity or during 1970s. Economic decline, War and Emergency disturbed the nation during this time. The sense of the same was reflected through a very thin stream of creativity. This period remains as a memory lane where the writers' of the next generation would visit and revisit.

The next breaking point in Indian Writing in English came with the publication of *Salman Rushdie's Midnight's Children* which went on to win the Booker McConnell Prize in 1981. The publication of Midnight's Children in 1981 is considered to be a harbinger of renaissance in Indian writing in English. Certain elements of postmodernism, experiments with language and grammar, focus on history, liveliness of language. Innovations through magic realism and allegory, references to contemporary Hindi cinema all made a smooth entry to the world of Indian English novel with Rushdie's highly influential novel. The language, style, theme and narrative technique employed by Rushdie is entirely original and highly innovative. He initiated a trend which cared very less about the continental method of writing novels. Incredible imagination, amazing comic sense and absolute word - play are the hallmarks of Rushdie's works. After 1980, the novel flourished incredibly in themes, use of language, style and technique. Writers like *Rohinton*

Mistry, Amitav Ghosh, ShashiTharoor, Arundhati Roy, Kiran Desai Vikram Seth have set their premise of writings around various socio-political and cultural issues that emerged in post independent India and rapidly changing Indian life; the social-political, cultural issues of a young multicultural democratic nation and their impact on communities and an individual's life. After*Rushdie*, the novel had been successfully worked out by the writers like Amitav Gosh with his novels like *The Circle reason, The Shadow Lines* and *The Glass Palace. ShashiTharoor* captured the political scenario in The Great 1ndia Novel while *Rohinton Mistry* focused on the scams in banks when banks in India underwent transformation and were getting nationalized and the impact of the same on Paris community. In 1990, *RohintanMisty's Such a Long Journey* was short listed for the Booker Prize. On the other hand *Vikram Seth's A Suitable Boy* accompanied by never before seen marketing drive in India in 1994. The New York Times (16 December 199 I) has called these new Indian writers *'Rushdie's children'*. These writers incorporate vibrant, pungent and colourful style of writing. Their use of Indian words seemed to be tingled with English language. The most noteworthy thing in their writing was the portrayal of India through the language which was a second language for them. Moreover India being a vast and diverse cultural country creates some additional problems like problems of expression. Nevertheless, Indian "Titers in English find the way out and showed an emerging India in their literary works. The common theme of Indianness binds them together. Along with this common theme their urban sensibility and ability to adopt the English language put them to the international credit. This generation of authors attar 1980 were relieved off the burden of the consciousness of both English language and novel as a form as something that belonged to the west. These novelists use English language deftly, covering a larger canvass of emotional, political, cultural, geographical and historical issues. There is an awareness of national and international developments reflected in themes woven around the displaced, marginalized modern man and uninhibited modifications in the genre. There is gusto of creativity, vigor, hope and confidence surfacing through rich, mischievous language, light -sometimes funny, comic and humorous approach that reigns their writing.

Indian English fiction underwent some changes of theme and setting. The theme of Indianness bought the element of nostalgia in their writings. The writings seemed to be memoirs or quasi-fictionalized memoirs, travelogues or inspired in part by real -life experiences and in part by writer's imagination. Contextually, these were the writer's critic of western based but having Indian origin or possibly the children of British Raj era-born and brought up in India and then migrated to the West. They exhibited the theme of nostalgia by romanticizing theirchildhood which they passed in the nation. They tried to relocate and rediscover the past experiences at India. In a way they indirectly advocated the national spirit with the emergence of innovative writing techniques. Thus, their contribution to the Indian writing in English was enormous. Their works have noticeably recognized and rapidly stands in the world market. In this way Indian writing in English has certainly expanded its scope throughout the world. The writer of Indian origin manifests India in their works with a great zeal. Their writings were often less-self-conscious and more light hearted and most probably concerning with impressionistic memories of place and people of the nation. Thus, they created a sign of long distant Nationalism.

In such a context of Realism on the background of urbanized setting, the arrival of *Chetan Bhagat* with his debut novel *Five Point Someone* in 2004 proved to be a revolutionary wave in the Indian Writing in English. A complete stranger to the literary establishment, *Bhagat* was an investment banker in Hong Kong. The novel, pioneering in devising a new genre of Indian Writing in English, was autobiographical in nature and portrayed the lives of three students at Ill' who found it difficult to deal with the traditional education system, with sparklinghumour and profound understanding. The fiction became a phenomenal success in the literary world with its sale of more than two hundred thousand copies. It dramatically changed the landscape of India's domestic publishing scenario by expanding the readership of English novels beyond the miniscule, metropolitan, highbrow elite and reached out to the unassuming, urban middle class India and, more importantly, to the youth of the nation.

The novel *Five Point someone* was rejected by many publishers before it was accepted by Rupa Publication. It threw gauntlet to the elitist view of literature which resonated only within the charmed circle of literary establishment that was dominated by hair-splitting critics and conceited academics. Indian English fictions before *Bhagat* were wealthy. They have *Naipauls, Seths, KushwantSinghs and Arundhati Rays*. But *Chetan Bhagat* has actualized something all these established authors were not able to. The common Indian has never been a zealous reader. The only digestible reading material they had were news tabloids and film magazines. Earlier Indian authors were considered too sophisticated to be understood by the common man. Earlier Indian English novels are heavy and hard on eyes and brain and usually deal with extremely serious subjects. Only elite readers, scholars and academicians had the privilege to read novels. But *Bhagat with Five Point Someone*, single handedly brought forth a revolutionary change in the entire scenario. Now there comes a refreshing type of novel: comparatively short, written in easy-to-read language, about everyday life and problems of today's young people. And it has all the cool and masala stuff thrown in good measures-coffee shops, malls, misery, alcohol, sex, poverty and so on. Bhagat got today's mall-going, bear drinking, so called traditional-Indian-value-breaking young Indians to buy paperback novels (often pirated ones) and read them.

The amazing sale of bhagat's novel surprised the publishing industry. Bhagat's*Five Point Someone* is a turning point of Indian English Fiction and marks the emergence of a new brand of Indian Fiction in English. Some critics, however, initially brushed off Bhaga!'s success as a fluke but his lasting popularity with his consequent novels like *One Night @ the Call Center, Three Mistakes of My Life, Two States and Revolution 2020* proved them wrong. All the books have remained bestsellers since their release and four of them have inspired Hollywood films like Hello, 3 Idiots. Kai Po Chef and 2 States Bhagat is now considered to be a youth icon and has been labeled as the 'Voice of New Generation' for the young, emerging urban middle class Indians.

CHAPTER SIX

Chetan Bhagat as a Post-Modernist Writer

Postmodern literature is a form of literature which is marked, both stylistically and ideologically, by a reliance on such literary conventions as fragmentation, paradox, unreliable narrators, often unrealistic and downright impossible plots, games, parody, paranoia, dark humor and authorial self-reference. Postmodern authors tend to reject outright meanings in their novels, stories and poems, and, instead, highlight and celebrate the possibility of multiple meanings, or a complete lack of meaning, within a single literary work. Postmodern literature also often rejects the boundaries between 'high' and 'low' forms of art and literature, as well as the distinctions between different genres and forms of writing and storytelling.

Post modernism in Indian English Literature refers to the works of literature after 1980. If Raja Rao's *Kanthapura (*1938) Marks Modernism, Salman Rushdie's *Midnight Children* (1981) And Nissim Ezekiel's *Latter-Day Psalms* (1982). Chetan Bhagat is an icon of new India and he has an enduring name in the ground of postmodern fiction. He has opened the floodgates for a new movement of Postmodernism in Indian Writing in English. His name doesn't grace any awards list, but he is familiar to every college student in India. While the global literary dwell on the fiction of India's past, Chetan Bhagat has become India's well known writer by embracing the present. He manages to retain his sense of humour even though the topics that are actually harsh realities of life.

His writing has revolutionized and mirrored the postmodern literature. According to him, the purpose of literature is to showcase the society. His works personal belongings and justifies how Chetan Bhagat is considered to be the postmodernist writer which is clearly documented by his own works.

Chetan Bhagat as Post-modernist:

As on date he has compiled six fictions and two non-fictions and in fact in every work he has highlighted his profound concern for the youth of today; i.e. the problems and despairs, hopes and aspirations of the youth. In spite of dealing with the unsympathetic realities of life his works administer to retain the pure sense of humor. His works have striking similarities with parables in projecting moral messages, divine guidance and technical suggestions. Along with that his works can better be defined as postmodern projection of parables due to the above reasons. The victories and defeats of the youth are common aspects of Chetan's stories with respect to the present generation and era. Hence, the present paper is based on those issues only. Yatri D. Dave in her insightful article, Culture of Consumerism as Reflected in Chetan Bhagat's *One Night @ the Call Center*, focuses the trends and techniques of modern world. She examines that the novel deals with Consumerism which shows how to attract customers while selling their products.

Chetan Bhagat (born 22nd of April, 1974) is a distinguished Indian author, a prolific writer, a noted columnist, a well – known screenwriter, and a motivational speaker, recognized for his English – language dramedy novels about young urban middle-class Indians. Chetan Bhagat is a luminary in the postmodern Indian fiction which revolves round hopes and despairs, smiles and tears, fears and cheers, happiness and sorrow, ambition and tribulation, love and separation of the youth of new India.

Chetan's style of writing is simple, lucid and vivid with graphic descriptions and linear narratives. Most of the protagonists in his novels are named after Lord Krishna such as Shyam, Krishna, Hari, Govind and Madhav.Bhagat is considered a youth icon rather than being just an author. With his vigorous and humorous way of depicting stories, he has encouraged the habit of reading in many young Indians. According to him, novels are perfect devices for both inspiration and entertainment and through which he disseminates his views and opinion about society and youth.

CHAPTER SEVEN

Chetan Bhagat as a Realistic Writer

Chetan Bhagat is a far cry from the typical author image that lies in the mind of the common man. He is dealing with the harsh realities of life and the problems faced by the young generation in his works. He holds a mirror to the society that gives the reflection of his own country and its perspectives. He writes for common people. The novels of Chetan Bhagat revolve around the world of Indian middle class, the real force behind India's economic growth, where lies the secret of his success also. He has revealed what he or the persons familiar to him have experienced in real life and the margins of fiction and real life blurs in his novels.

The secret of Chetan Bhagat's success is his selection of topics that are common. He selects subjects which the readers can associate with a mix of sentiment, romance, relationship, religion and politics and also has social message. The unique things of his fictions are sensitive issues addressed in the most rational way. His novels are the portrayal of dreams and aspirations of all characters and the characters seem more real, simple and genuine. He has written in simple English with no frills. One may suggest that Chetan Bhagat is working on well thought format that he has included numbers in all the title of his book like 'Five', 'One', 'Two' and 'Three' or may show his superstition to add number in the titles.

He is the front runner of these new types of authors who do not use heavy duty English instead he uses just simple spoken English in India. Indian sentiments, passions, friendship, love, religion, cricket and happy endings are given in his novels that cite the Indianism. India is well known for its varied cultural heritage as it is known for the sparkling and traditionally various marriages. Chetan Bhagat has explored in different ways in all the three books. Highlighting various aspects of the country, he has followed a pattern with his books by naming the protagonists after "Lord Krishna", he has named his characters Hari, Syam, Govind and Krishna. His writing style is largely similar in all the four novels, till date. However, it is seen that the seriousness of the novels gradually goes on increasing. Each novel has the basic character set.

The protagonist is a very normal kind of boy whom any Indian teenager can easily identify in terms of thoughts and view. However, the disbeliever attitude of the lead character in **Three Mistakes** is an exception. Besides, a special importance to sex is given in each of his books. The friends of the protagonist are also of very common nature. The girls in the novels are shown in virtual bondage by their respective families. Yet, the girls can be easily compared to an average Indian girl. Thus, the novel has no supernatural characters and is really set in a typical Indian setting and also all typical neighborhood characters. This admixture of humour and pathos, hopes, aims and fears and success and failure brands his work.

His novels have great quantity of that quality which generally absent in many of the so called famous authors. His books may not rank as the greatest, but they, no doubt, are far ahead of them in popularity. **Five Point Someone** is Chetan Bhagat's first novel which was published in 2004. This novel has fictionalized his IIT experiences with the touch of love and comedy. By the very first work itself, he could make a mark in the realms of Indian English fiction. Chetan Bhagat focuses on the lives of three friends of IIT (Delhi) Hari Kumar (the narrator), Alok Gupta and Ryan Obero. The trio suffers ridicule of the teachers as well as the classmates.

However, they stay to reform the ancient system of education. They dislike the teaching method, which is as old as the college itself. The students are asked to mug the subjects in order to score good grades. Bhagat puts an emphasis on the observational teaching. It must support them to apprehend the things in a natural way.

The Three Mistakes of My Life, his third novel, centers round politics and riots which are not unfamiliar to India at any point of time. The novel **The Three Mistakes of My Life** mainly focuses on the innovative ideology and the motives of three friends. It touches an emotional chord of the third generation of India. His novel displays the ambition of the youth which is mixed with fears and tinged with tears. The narrator sees massacre as the huge loss of national property. This is the virtue of the novel that distinguishes it from others that the novelist finds only a human being in the people of all religions.

The Three Mistakes of My Life depicts Gujarat and Gujarati youth representing not only a particular region but making a youth representing a whole country and its enthusiastic folk. Chetan depicts how the mind of the modern youth is affected by some problems of the country and contemporary issues.It deals with the young Indians' trial and troubles in their life. Modern young generation and its reactions to the political, social and personal issues are the main concern of the novelist. Youth is the important section of the society who is supposed to build the nation. Govind, Ish and Omiare three best friends and are the central characters in the novel that represent the developing part of Ahmadabad and have different passions in their lives namely business, cricket and religion. Business, Cricket and Religion are the three crucial factors which play a significant role in Indian scenario.

The idea of starting some business as a joint venture becomes successful. The cricket shop started by these three friends is running very well. The novelist has included many of the issues that Gujarat and India have ultimately faced, like severe earthquake in Bhuj on 26th Jan '2001andGodhra Mishap of 27th Feb '2002, and the grim condition thereafter with communal riots as its consequence.

What exactly is the reaction of young generation is caught by the author? Human emotions are showed very realistically. Truly, **The Three Mistakes of My Life** is a real insight into 21st century experiences of Indian youth. He has proved himself to be the writer of the masses. The three passions of three friends are actually the passions of Indian youth. The real life events like the Gujarat earthquakes, India-Australia Cricket series and Gujarat riots are cleverly woven into the story which makes it more relevant to their regular life.

ChetanBhagat, in his novel **2 States: The story of My Marriage** deals with a very serious theme in a light way. This novel definitely gives the readers some cultural shocks. This novel projects the true spirit of nationalism. It is based on the social and sentimental endeavours of the two main characters Ananya Swaminathan and Krish Malhora, which attempts to unite not only two states but also two traditions and cultures and has touched some of the sensitive issues of cultural differences, father-son relationship and corporate exploitation. He has viewed that love knows no boundaries, whether it is out of caste, creed, religion, states or countries. To some extent, this story seems to be of ChetanBhagat's own, but he has never claimed it. It's definitely love that triumphs against all odds. **2 States: The story of My Marriage** is a story of inter-state marriage in India. And it is a love story of a Punjabi guy Krish, and a Tamil Brahmin girl Ananyain his own style. Many families undergo such circumstances in India. This novel is about his own love marriage and the obstacles faced by the protagonists, his wife and himself coming from different regions of India. Chetan Bhagat conveys what happens when two worlds meet very well.

The story begins in the IIM Ahmadabad mess, where Krish, a Punjabi boy from Delhi sights a beautiful girl, Ananya, a Tamil from Chennai, quarreling with the mess staff about the food. They become friends within a few days and decide to study together every night. In time, they become romantically involved. They both get good jobs, and have serious plans for their wedding. At first Krish tries to convince his girlfriend Ananya's parents and at last he convinces them by helping Anaya's father to do his first PPT and later convinces her mom by arranging for her an opportunity to sing in a big concert organized by Krish's office. She is convinced and turns happy for has her biggest dream of singing in a big concert has come true. Then, they try to convince Krish's mother where the problem is Krish's relatives who don't like this type of inter-state marriage. They say that Krish should not marry a Madrasi but end up agreeing with them when Ananya tries to help one of Krish's cousins to get married and succeeds in doing so.

Now, as they have convinced both their parents, they try to make their parents meet each other to get to know. They go to Goa. But this dream of theirs ends as Ananya's parents find something fishy between Krish's mom and him. Anaya's family ends up deciding that Krish and Ananyacan not marry each other. At last Krish's father who is like an enemy for Krish helps Ananya to get married as he convinces Ananya's family well. His own real life events are cleverly rushed into the story which makes it more relevant to his regular life. He realizes that the characters in the novel discreetly become part of his own life.

This paper may reveal the concept of realism and concept of modernity and how through the delineation of the various characters of Chetan Bhagat, these are portrayed in the contemporary reality. He has always expressed himself in a way which is understood by all and every generation can connect itself to it. His thoughts are worded in such a skillful way that they are understood by readers instantly. His language is so enjoyable that it flows smoothly without any burden of being metaphysical. The tone of the author towards his readers is also worth mentioning. He shows a conversational understanding throughout the narration and is not an outsider in the story. The lack of distance between the reader and author is one of the reasons for the greater fascination for his novels among the readers. Chetan Bhagat has always presented a true picture of life in India in his novels which always makes him a realistic writer.

CHAPTER EIGHT

A Critical Comment on Chetan Bhagat Selected novels

Chetan Bhagat popularity lays his ability to hit the right chord in youth. The major attractions in his books are the theme that students all over the country can relate to. From a literary point of view, he does not belong to the league of Vikram Seth or Arundhati Roy. So far he writes these books which the youngish take to as fish would to water. ChetanBhagat has truly been a trend setter giving rise to the culture of campus novels in India. Hence, the Indian English novel has gained a viability, enthusiasm and vitality, attracting a remarkably wide readership and universal praise, to which the new novelists have made a positive contribution.

Critical Commands

Chetan Bhagat is a far cry from the typical author image that lies in the minds of the common men. He deals with the harsh realities of life and problems faced by the young generation in his work. Chetan Bhagat's most outstanding quality as a novelist is his simple, transparent, and plain language which even a secondary grade student can simply comprehend. His language is so enjoyable that it flows smoothly without any burden of metaphysical or existential philosophies and even a layman can follow his world of fiction where reading does not become a boring make an effort which only the academic choice can participate.

The novels of Chetan Bhagat turn around the middle class those applications ambitions, worries, as well as the sad predicament of the middle class are described with an omniscient insider's view in his novels. Being a member of the same level of the society, he is enlightening what he or people familiar to him have experienced in real life and the margins of fiction and real life shape in his novels. The corruption, unemployment, the grasping attitudes of the elder generation, the superficial love- hate relationships amongst the youths are some of the various themes that he has discussed in his novels. The chief principles and ethics of Indian democracy which are really on the cross roads at present because of the all distributing corruption and self-critical tendencies in the society and the protest of middle class for the sorry state of relationships of the country can also be seen in his novels.

The quality of the author towards his readers is also worth mentioning. He shows a conversational understanding towards his readers throughout the explanation. He is not unknown in the tale, but in all of his novels can identify the presence of a man who went through all of the parallel situations what he describes. The lack of distance between the reader and author is one of the reasons for the greater fascination for his novels among the readers.

The secret success for Chetan Bhagat is the selection of topics that are common. He chooses theme that the readers can associate with his novel with a mix of sentiment, romance, relationship, religious and politics, Indian sentiments, Passions, Friendship, Love, Cricket and happy ending, and also has social message that the unique thing about his fictions are sensitive issues are addressed in the most normal way. His strong narration has people relating to situations, incidents and characters in a neutral way. His novels talk about dreams and aspirations of all characters and characters seemed more real and simple genuine fears. He has written in simple English with no trimmings. Chetan Bhagat has some kind software, which he uses to write his novel. He just puts new character's names, situations in the software and the characteristic of his protagonist is parallel, their thoughts procedure is also like. One more thing which recommend that Chetan Bhagat is working on well thought format is that he included numbers in all the title of his book **'Five', 'One', 'Two' and 'Three'** or may be it in his superstition to add number in the titles, who don't use heavy duty English instead he used just simple spoken English in India. India is well known for it is varied cultural heritage as it is known for the sparkling and traditionally different matrimony. Chetan Bhagat explored indifferent ways in all the four books. He highlights various aspects of the country. He has followed a pattern with his books by naming the protagonists. After **"Lord Krishna" Hari, Syam, Govind** and **Krishna** and also has used number in the titles of each books. His writing style is basically similar in all his novels, till date, however, it is seen that the seriousness of the novels gradually went on increasing in each novel has set the basic character. The central character is a very ordinary type of young man with whom any Indian teenager can easily reacted to his moderate in terms of thoughts and view and is not to firm. The protagonists of friends are also of very general nature. The girls' character of his novels are shown in virtual bondage by their respective families and the girls can be simply compared to an average Indian girl. Thus, the novel has no supernatural characters and is really set in a typical Indian setting and also all typical neighborhood characters. This admixture of humor and pathos, hopes, aims and fears and success and failure brands his work.

His two novels has become story line for two blockbuster movies: **"Five Point Some One" in the name of "3 idiots" and "One Night @ the Call Center" in the name of "Hello"**. We can expect more such wonders from him.

His novels have great quantity of that quality which is generally absent in many of called infamous authors. His books may not rank as the greatest; **"Five Point Some One"** is Chetan Bhagat's first novel which was published in 2004. This novel has fictionalized experience of his IIT with handle of love and comedy. By the first attempt itself, he could complete spot in the realms of Indian

English literature. Chetan Bhagat focuses on the lives of three friends of IIT (Delhi) Hari Kumar (the storyteller), Alok Gupta and Ryan Oberoi. The trios go through ridicule of the teachers as well as the colleagues. While, they want to reform the old system of educational training, they hate the teaching technique, which is as old as the academy itself. The pupils are asked to mug the subject matter in order to score good grades. Chetan Bhagat puts stress on the study. The author believes this technique must help the students in receiving clear of mugging. It must support them to capture perception the natural way. His novel deals with the life of the three friends whose relation on making it to one of the best engineering colleges in Indian. It is quickly depressed by the firmness and monotony of academic work.

His second novel, **"One night @ the call center"**, the analysis and troubles of the life of call center employees. He exposes harsh truth life about call centers employees by this novel. It is a dark park which can't be seen by anyone else even they can relate to regular life to any characters in this novel. The story described in such a way that it looks more like a film rather than a novel and is a flashback in the book. The writer chooses to describe it through the eyes of central character. He brings about a great shift in the style of writing wants to explore globalization. The entire novel is divided into two parts. All characters live mechanized lives. The novelist describes family issues, problems of work place etc., in a genuine and interesting way. **'One Night @ the Call Center'** brings modern culture in India. The themes involve the anxieties and insecurities of the rising Indian middle class people, including questions about profession, family conflicts in a shifting India attitude, and the friendship of the young Indian middle class to both executives and ordinary clients whom they serve in the U.S.A. It's the story of a group of people working at a call center. All of them have individual troubles in life, however, they are friends rather than colleagues working together. Their call center is under the threat of closure mainly because of the economic slowdown and other reasons. 'They are our country's most productive western culture'. It is true in the context of Bhagat's novel too. Even after the fall down of the British Empire, the domination of the Whiteman continues most prominently the American call centers dominate India. As seen in **One Night @ Call Center**, the Indians at call centers work all night for their white masters on the other side of the globe. Bill Gate's **Microsoft** has given a new avatar to the third countries especially India. Now these computers have colonized as Indian people .Cheta nBhagat narrates the episode of 'God' when all characters are at climax when they are near to death. The characters apparently listen to their inner voice and suggest them the way on that they are moving irresponsible and not successful. There is no network but there is a call from God and after that there is a radical change in everybody's life. The end novel deals with reformation of all characters.

"The Three Mistakes of My Life", his third novel, centers round politics and religious riots which is not unfamiliar to India at any point of time. The novel '3 Mistakes' mainly focuses on the innovative ideology and the motives of 3 friends. It is touching an emotional triad of the third generation of India. His novel displays the ambition of the youth which is mixed with fears and tinged with tears. The storyteller sees mass destruction as the enormous loss of national assets. **The Three Mistakes of My Life** depicts Gujarat and Gujarati youth representing not only a particular region but also making a youth representing a whole country and its enthusiastic folk. Chetan depicts how the mind of the modern youth has been affected by some problems of the country and contemporary issues. It deals with the young Indians' trial and troubles in their life. Modern young generation and its reactions to the political, social and personal issues are the main concerns of the novelist. Youth is the important section of the society who is supposed to build the nation. Govind, Ish and Omi are the three best friends and are the central characters in the novel that represent the developing part of Ahamadabad and have different passions in their lives namely business, cricket and religion. Business, Cricket and Religion are the three crucial factors which play a pivotal role in Indian scenario.

This is the virtue of the novel that distinguishes it from others that the novelist finds only a human being in the people of all religious. This admixture of humor and pity, hopes and fears and success and failure brands his work blockbuster but dark comedies of third generation in India. Bhagat's The 3 Mistakes of My Life is a novel of the dark passion. It records the sexual boldness of the woman protagonist. Tree friends unite together to preserve the national aptitude. The first time an Indian writer has elevated his characters about the touch of the society such as asterism, religion and worship.

In the fourth novel **"2 States: The story of My Marriage"**, describes the true patriotism, it is support on the social order and idealistic performance of two main characters AnanyaSwaminathan and KrishMalhotra. This novel attempts to bring together two states and civilization and society. These activities to point out the people of the country only as Indians not as community, religions, society, culture and circumstances etc., "2 States the story of my marriage" is a own life story of author. The problems of central character had presented to face to marry a girl from the south Indian that clearly give details the south – north Indian divided into culture and attitudes of people although how much they are civilized. '2 ***States the story of my marriage*** gives absolutely cultural shocks and serious theme. Chetan Bhagat touched some of the sensitive issues of cultural variation, father-son relationship, cross-culture conflict and corporate utilization and love know no limitations, whether it is to be statement of belief, community, religion, state or country. It's a story of inter-state marriage in India, a love story of a Punjabi boy **Krish**, and a Tamil Brahmin girl **Ananya.** Many families go through this situation in India. This novel is about love marriage and difficulty between two main characters and is reflections his wife faced coming from different regions of India. The novel is interpreted in different perspectives and of love marriage and its problems in Indian context with other social problems. Chetan Bhagat's writing along with the way in which he presented his characters. It also talks about the concept of realism and concept of modernity and how through the delineation of the various characters Chetan Bhagat portrays the contemporary reality. Chetan Bhagat's novels touch an emotional chord of the modern generation of India. Young generations are stayed from morality and their only motto in life is – eat, drink, and enjoy life. Behind their happiness, existential trouble is hidden about their future and unrelenting presence of their past. Two generations after independence, one of the essential characteristics of the new India is that the educated middle class who once turned to English for trade applications now see it in a dissimilar culture. He has bare thoughts and expose to harsh realities of life and modern life of young generation and problem faced by the young generation in his works etc. He brings about corporate culture is a term used to describe beliefs and a value system that provides its unique taste and attitude to a friendship in Cosmo-culture the condition of youth is very pathetic. In this world of Cosmo-culture, everybody is involved in an extra marital relationship. He carefully selects subject which the reader can associate with modern culture.

Each of his novels has the basic character set. The Protagonist is a very normal kind of boy whom any Indian teenager can easily relate to. He is moderate in terms of thoughts and views and is not to assertive. However the atheist attitude of the lead character in Three Mistakes is an exception. Besides, a special importance to sex is given in each of his books. The friends of the Protagonist are also of very common nature. The girls in the novels are shown in virtual bondage by their respective families. Yet even the girls can be easily compared to an average Indian girl. Thus, his novel has no peculiar characters and is really set in a typical Indian setting.

Conclusion

Chetan Bhagat has always tried to touch upon something new. His writing always seen close to reality. He has spoken himself in a way that is understood by all and every generation can connect itself to it. His thoughts are said to be a statement in such a clever way that they are understood by readers right away. Chetan Bhagat has always presented a true picture of life in India by him novels.

He is one of the most popular contemporary Indian novelists in English. Chetan Bhagat's writing along with the way in which he presented his characters. He also discusses the concept of social reflection and concept of modernity and how through the delineation of the various characters chetan Bhagat portrays the contemporary reality. As a writer, he is gifted with an extraordinary ability to deal with various aspects of human life. His popularity as a writer rests basically on his intimate understanding of human nature. He is an outstanding writer who concentrates on the passion of the people and deals with them from different perspectives. His novel deals with different colors of passion such as love, anger, hatred, and faith, which makes it more relevant to our regular life. This novel tells us that the characters unnoticeably become part of our own life. Its amusing style and easy language charm our mind. He has always expressed himself in a way which in understood by all and every generation can connect itself to it. His thoughts are worded in such a skillful way that they are understood by readers instantly. Chetan Bhagat books have always presented a true picture of life in India.

CHAPTER NINE

A Study on Narrative strategies in Chetan Bhagat selected novels

Chetan Bhagat is an emerging author an Indian English Literature. His arrival in the world of Indian English Fiction coincided with a time when the presence of a vibrant media culture and the growth of a corporate structure in the urban and semi-urban Indian society was effecting changes in the reading tastes, especially for the younger generation whose incorporation into the corporate design were only increasing. He is a far cry from the typical author image that lies in the mind of the common man. He is dealing with the harsh realities of life and problems faced by the young generation in his work. He holds a mirror to society and presents the reflection of the society of our own country.

The secret success for ChetanBhagat is selection of topics which are common. He selects subjects which the readers can associate with his novel with a mix of sentiment, romance, relationship, religions and politics. His strong narration has people relating to situations, incidents and characters in a natural way. His novel talks about dreams and aspirations of all characters and character seemed more real and simple genuine reservations. His narratives often lean towards the dramatic. The dramatic element is prominent, as Bhagat chose to begin his tales with 'prologues' which either contains the dramatic tell- alls as in***'2 States-The story of my marriage'*** or compose the most dramatic episode of the book as in ***'One Night @ the Call Center'***. His 'acknowledgements' are no less dramatic, which often betrays his anxious attempt of highlighting his 'product' as a innovative and better brand, such as his claims in the "Acknowledgements" to '***Three Mistakes of my Life'*** that he does not "want to be Indian's most admired writer", he "wants to be India's most loved writer", or his providing the readers with a questionnaire in ***One Night @ the Call Center.*** Again his novels are called "Acts" and his endings "Epilogues". Not only the dramatic, but he plentifully draws his techniques from the cinematic form as well. His narrative a swing naturally back and forth using the 'flash-back' technique and his language is very lucid and easy to understand too that is largely in sync with fast narrative is full of what is called 'chutnified' expressions, inter-language code-switching which is common on the Internet circuit. Besides this deliberate patterning of the narrative and the diction approach towards the issues, he addresses is part of his wonderful arrangement skill. As for the narrative, Bhagat resorts to the thriller and the fantastic form and also his novel deals with a very serious theme in a light way.

Liberty

In the viewpoint of the novelist, a Libertarian is always straight forward in his approach to life and listens to the voice of his soul which he strongly believes in, is ever true. He may suffer a big loss but finally emerges out victorious. In his novels, ChetanBhagat exhibits uncurbed spirits of the young people of his nation. In his first novel, '***Five Point someone'***, **Ryan, Alok and Hari** fight against the patriarchal education system, run by the old educationists. The education system of IIT Delhi depicted in his book is adhered to the same patriarchal norms and codes of education. The student's life could be shared if he was liberated to choose the study of his own choice. The novelist advises the youths not to make race with others but with themselves if they want to succeed in life.

In the second novel ***'One Night @ the Call Center'***, the novelist introduces characters with five advocates of individual liberty viz. **Shyam, Vroom, Priyanka, Esha and Radhika.** They are living with family marginalization. They want live liberty: A Libertarian follows and asks others to follow the four things to success: "One a medium amount of Intelligence and Two, a bit of imagination... the Third thing you need for success is self-confidence... The fourth part is most painful one". And it is something all of them still need to learn.

In the third novel ***'The 3 Mistakes of my Life'*** the novelist introduce characters with three libertarians' viz., **Govind, Ishan and Omi.** Ishan strongly believes in the virtues of humanity and loves the people of all community equally. The author believes "Humanity wouldn't have progressed if people listened to their parents all the time". (103) and suggests the youths to act upon the call of their self. The author criticizes politics and religion too. He evokes youth to keep religion far away from politics if they are truly religious. ChetanBhagat ignites the qualities of liberty in the youths. He calls them up to prefer human values to all other routine things. They should develop libertarian out-look to judge values of the human beings. This is the libertarian outlook of ChetanBhagat which follows not only through all his novels but also through his blood vessels. He thinks freely, writes freely and believes in the freedom of self and that of others. He writes against the corrupt system and suggests how to eliminate its impurities.

Chetan Bhagat's fourth novel in ***'2 States: The story of my Marriage'*** deals with a very serious theme in a high way. This novel definitely gives us cultural shocks. ChetanBhagat has touched some of the sensitive issues of cultural differences, father-son relationship and corporate exploitation. He is of the view that love knows no boundaries, whether it be of caste, creed, religion, states or countries. To some extent, this story seems to be of ChetanBhagat, but he never claimed it. It's definitely love that triumphs against all chances. It's a story of inter-state marriage in India, a love story of a Punjabi boy **Krish**, and a Tamil Brahmin girl **Ananya.** Many families go through his condition in India. This novel is about love marriage and the obstacles between protagonist and his wife faced coming from different regions of India. The interpretation of novel is interpreted in different perspective. The novel is explored and explained with understanding different perspectives of love marriage and its problems in Indian context with other social problems.

Representing youth Culture and Globalization

ChetanBhagat has explored youth culture and their issues in his novels. His novels depicted youth's world, their culture, challenges, problems, addictions, parties, fast foods, fashions, tastes, interests, attitudes, relationships, love, expectations, responsibilities, nationalism, disloyalty, stress and their various complexes. In addition is found college-life-culture, sick education system, demanding exams and canteen-chats, movie goings, ragging and fresher-senior classification. His two novels have autobiographical elements. The author has keen interest in 'yoga', which reflected as a unique and spiritual theme. The biblical concept **'Believe in thyself'** is there in the first novel. It questions whether high grades are important than other aspects of life. ***'One Night @ the Call Center'*** also made us to meditate on concept like **'Inner Call'** and links it with phone call majestically.

ChetanBhagat is representing nothing about remote India, the rural youth and their issues in this novel, though having different social background, have equal opportunities to them in education jobs friendship for example: the youth of former novel study in IIT and youth in later novel work in call center and games etc. The youth from Indian remote places have no much awareness of all these transformations. Corporate culture is a term, used to describe beliefs and a value system that provides its unique essence and attitude to a company. In Cosmo-culture, the condition of youth is very pathetic. Everywhere, he finds exploitation, frustration, rejection and like this. In this world, of Cosmo-culture, everybody is involved in an extra marital relationship. Today in India, youngster may keep unsocial hours, neglects his family obligations, drink excessive cocktails and date each other with a casualness that horrifies parents. Everybody wants high salary, fashionable life style; they are our country's most productive generation. ChetanBhagat has succeeded to revel nothing but the youth culture of India and some of their issues, who considers it his responsibility to appeal the young generation in Indian by writing a novel based on the Call Center etc. Which is a gift of globalization? Although Call Center is considered as a boon for India which is facing the problem of unemployment, ChetanBhagat's highlights the influence of call center, which is a globalization on the personal social, moral, intellectual and cultural relations of the Call Center employees. In India, normally Call Center employees have to work throughout the night to deal with the western customers. One of the bright sides of globalization is that Indian youth are getting good job opportunities in Western Countries.

His novel also focuses on how the young people while running after their career, are forgetting their duty towards parents. Through the example of the military uncle..., ChetanBhagat touches the clash between the **'old and modern'** with the changing atmosphere. The youth population is enormous and is growing at a fast rate. Every year, more people are educated and more Indians have got good opportunity to compete globally. This locked up potential can be given free expression only if the youth have someone to act as their role-model: a person who can organize and guide the masses towards a common goal; someone who can inspire and motivate them for their success.

Conclusion

ChetanBhagat is a far cry from the typical author image that lies in the mind of the common man. He is dealing with the harsh realities of life and problems faced by the young generation in his work. He holds a mirror to society and presents the reflection of the society of our own country. He writes for common people. His language is very lucid and easy to understand and on dark topics, still hold some humour in it. Chetan Bhagat's books are light and breezy and the language is simple. The author uses a lot of can't words that Indians use every day. The narrative of the story stays fresh though, the ending of the story is expected, still find characters rooting for the lead characters to get together at the end. Bhagat is narrative do **'reflect and deals'** neither **"technically nor thematically**" form. His strong narration has people relating to situations, incidents and characters in a natural way. His novel talks about dreams and aspirations of all characters and character seemed more real with simple genuine fears. In his narrative capability he is looked upon as a pioneer of the new form which is perfectly fit to bring about the issues of the multilingual generation.

CHAPTER TEN

Socio-Scientific issues as found in Chetan Bhagat's "one night @ the call center"

As the title implies socio scientific issues in Chetan Bhagat's '**One night @ the call center**', ChetanBhagat is a modern social fiction writer. He writes for common people and dark topics, modern life, education, information technology etc. His language is very lucid and easy to understand. In this novel, ChetanBhagat reveals harsh truths about call centers, a dark part which can't be seen by anyone else. Even we can relate our life to any character in the novel. The entire novel is divided into two parts. All characters live mechanized lives. The novelist describes family issue, problems of work place etc. in a genuine and interesting way. The second part of the novel deals with reformation of all characters.

Science Fiction is a genre of fiction dealing with imaginary but more or less reasonable content such as future settings, futuristic science and technology, space travel, aliens and paranormal abilities. Exploring the consequences of scientific innovations is one purpose of science fiction, making it "literature of ideas". Science Fiction is a largely based on writing rationally about alternative possible worlds or futures.

Definition of Science Fiction

Science Fiction is difficult to define, as it includes a wide range of subgenres and themes. Realistic speculation about possible future events based on adequate knowledge of the real world, past and present, and a thorough understanding of the nature and signification of the scientific method. The first science fiction fanzine, **The Comet,** was published in 1930. Fanzine printing methods have changed over the decades, from the hectograph, the mimeograph, and the ditto machine, to modern photocopying. The earliest organized fandom online was the Science Fiction, Lovers community, originally a mailing list in the late 1970s with a text archive filing that was updated regularly.

History

Science Fiction has antecedents back to mythology as a means of understanding the world through speculation and storytelling. Science fiction as literature can be seen in **Lucian's** True History in the 2nd century, some of the **Arabian Nights** tales, **The Tale of the Bamboo Cutter** in the 10th century, etc. A product of the budding Age of Reason and the development of modern science itself, **Jonathan Swift's Gulliver's Travels** was one of the first true science fantasy works. Following the 18th century development of the novel as a literary form. In the early s19th century, Mary Shelley's **books Frankenstein and the Last Man** helped define the form of the science fiction novel; later **Edgar Allan Poe** wrote a story about a flight to the moon. More examples appeared throughout the 19th century. In the late 19th century, the term "scientific romance" was used in Britain to describe much of this fiction. In the early 20th century, pulp magazines helped develop a new generation of mainly American SF writers, influenced by **Hugo Gernsback**, the founder of Amazing Stories Magazine. In the development of the World-Wide Web exploded the community of online fandom by orders of importance, with thousands and then literally millions of web sites devoted to science fiction and related genres for all media.

The term science fiction has entered popular culture, writers and fans active in the field came to associate the term with low-budget, low-tech "B-movies" and with low-quality pulp science fiction.

The innovation of science fiction has provided criticism of developing and future technologies; it also produces innovation and new technology. The discussion of this topic has occurred mire in literary and sociological than in scientific forums. Cinema and media theorist **VivainSobchack** examines the dialogue between science fiction film and the technological imagination. Technology impacts artists and how they portray their fictionalized subjects, but the fictional world gives back to science by enlargement imagination. While more common in the beginning years of science fiction with writers like **Arthur C.Clarke**, new authors still find ways to make the currently impossible technologies seem closer to being realized.

Kind of science fiction

Hard science fiction is characterized by rigorous attention to accurate detail in quantitative sciences, especially physics, astrophysics, and chemistry, or on accurately depicting worlds that more advanced technology may make possible.

The description **"soft" science fiction** may describe works based on social sciences such as psychology, economics, political science, sociology, and anthropology. Related to Social SF and Soft SF are the speculative fiction branches of **utopian** or **dystopian** stories. Aldous Huxley's **Brave New World** and Margaret Atwood's **The Handmaid's Tale** are examples. Satirical novels with fantastic settings such as **Gulliver's Travels** by Jonathan Swift may be considered speculative fiction.

Military science fiction is set in the context of conflict between national, interplanetary, or interstellar armed forces, the primary viewpoint characters are usually soldiers. **Space opera** is adventure science fiction set in outer space or on distant planets, where the emphasis is on action rather than either science or characterization. The conflict is heroic, and typically on a large scale. Space opera is sometimes used judgmentally, to describe improbable plots, absurd science, and cardboard characters.

The study of science fiction, or science fiction studies, is the critical assessment, interpretation, and discussion of science fiction literature, film, new media, fandom, and fan fiction. Science fiction scholars take science fiction as an object of study in order to better understand it and its relationship to science, technology, politics, and culture-at-large.

The Change of literature

It's often said that Science Fiction is the literature of change. When a culture is undergoing a lot of changes due to scientific advances and technological developments, and expects to undergo more. It's hardly surprising if stories about these changes become popular as a way of expressing people's feeling, 'this story must be set against a society significantly different from our own usually, but not necessarily, because of some change in the level of science and technology or it is not a science fiction story'. The science fiction story does not deal with the restoration of order, but with change and ideally, with continuing changes.

Socio-Political Conflict

The present paper is an attempt to study the impact of globalization in the selected works of ChetanBhagat. Likewise the modern stories by ChetanBhagat are based on the lifestyle in the I.T sector of Gurgaon and Bangalore.

The story is narrated in such a way that it looks more like a movie rather than a novel. Bhagat bringing about a radical change in the style of writing wants to explore globalization. Globalization means development in technology and business. That technology entered into market that is known as B.P.O. In India B.P.O flourished because we have manpower, affecting the youth of India to entire night. Due to call centers, every night all potential is wasted. All characters live mechanized lives in the call center. Consumerism is fallout of Globalization in the corporate world and this concept is reflected in this novel. With the advent of globalization, the scenario of the corporate world has become more of consumer centered or product centered. Consumerism means developing managerial skills, uplifting of a system, upgrading of technology, approach to the problem and immediate solution of problem and satisfaction of customer. In this novel, Bhagat criticizes our government and call centers in Vroom's voice:

"Our government doesn't realize this, but Americans are using us.

We are sacrificing an entire generation to service their call centers."

Bhagat determinedly draws parallels between United States behaviour and the behaviour of India's governmental and managerial elites.

. The call center is achieved by convincing United States customers of Western Computers, the firm that outsourcers its support to the Indian call center, that terrorist have attacked the United States with a computer virus that will do untold confusion upon the United States economy. Customers are persuaded of this fact by being encouraged to activate an in pulled testing script within Microsoft Word which results in the software generating page of text. They are than encouraged to repeatedly call the help line as a means of notifying authorities about the process of virus.

Vroom likens United States American military action to the behaviour of the call-center manager, Bakshi, and describes "the whole world [...] being run by a bad stupid-evil boss" (208). Likewise, United States overseas investments and employment practices are represented as demeaning and inequitable, so that Vroom also complains about Americans tossing "their loose change" at Indian workers (228) and decrying the reality.

The corrupt state of politicians in our country is mentioned in the novel, "Why don't politicians commit suicides?"A call center employs points out that even though housewives, businessmen, employees and film stars commit suicide but politicians never do so because they are never hurt, they don't feel anything and unfortunately this nation is run by people who do not feel anything. All call center employees slog night after night so that they can have some money with which they can realize their simple dreams like building nursery schools and the like. There is uncertainty in their jobs as their jobs are depending on their companies, their clients, in case other client companies fail they would also be negatively affected. The general feeling of call center employees is that Americans are successful because of their money power. As far as the call center jobs are concerned, call centers pay more, but only because the exchange rate is in the favor of the Americans and that they toss their loose change at us. It seems like a lot in rupees. But jobs that pay less could be better. There could be other jobs that define us, and make us learn or help our country. The fact is that money is not progress in building something lasting for the future.

Exploitation

All characters are exploited in the name of Globalization, but **Esha's and Radhika**husband's characters are replicas of globalization. Esha has compromised by sleeping with a designer to get a modeling contract. However the guy turned out to be opportunistic as he betrays her by telling her she can't become a model due to her height. He also tries to console her by sending her some money. Esha feels terribly betrayed and tries to suppress the mental pain by inflicting herself with physical pain by purposely cutting her skin. Vroom is shocked to learn that Bakshi has cheated him and Shyam by submitting their work as his own. To add to his miseries, he overhears Esha telling the other girls that she had slept with a designer to get a modeling contract. In this world of Cosmo Culture, everybody is involved in an extra marital relationship.

Radhika, who loved her husband very much, is shocked to learn about his dark side. When Vroom calls up her husband portraying as a radio jockey and asks him to dedicate roses and a song to someone special, he chooses his girlfriend Payal over his wife. Radhika who listens to this gets terribly upset as her husband has betrayed her. Radhika is a very faithful and innocent wife. She never ever complains to her husband regarding the misbehavior of her mother-in-law. She is very responsible too. So she does household activity during the day time and works at a call-center at night.

Mr.Bakshi exploits like anything, he puts aside ethics and all moral values just to grow up. He forgets his inner self too"Western Computers Troubleshooting Website, Project Details and user Manual Developed by Connexions in Delhi SubhashBakshi Manager, Connections... (P.145)." He had cheated Shyam and Vroom, by submitting the Troubleshooting Website to the Boston Center as his own without crediting Shyam or Vroom. Through this episode we can say that youth is hungry for success through issues. The novel ignores fundamental intra-national inequalities of class owing to its faith in the liberalizing potential of modern capitalism.

Psychological Issues

This is social disorder. Everybody is looking for money. Nowadays in the new generation, hungry generation, dialects, genres, gathering places, slang music, social class can be an important factor. Today in India youngster may keep unsocial hours, neglect his family obligations, drink excessive cocktails and date each other with a casualness that horrifies parents. Everybody wants high salary, fashionable life style. They are our country's most productive generation.

Everybody is working for social recognition, economical and even social status. People loss their culture and beliefs when they enter call center. Today everybody lives a material life. Every character is from the common people of society. The employees have no time for attending even cousin's or neighbor's weddings all that was of importance to them is to hop on to the Qualis to go to work because their philosophy is that "there is activism in chasing money too." The reason for chasing money is because they have cash. "...the only reason Americans have a say in this world is because they have cash." The day we get money we can win them over. So the first thing we have to do is get the money. The Call Center working at such places with no sense of self-worth but only money to goad you along is naturally depressing and the employees get over their frustration by visiting the dance floors in the malls: "Drinks, dance floors, loud jarring gay music, drunken fights, and a fight means a party is totally rocking." One has to strategic vision and managerial leadership and the like to do well in life. They were shallow with no emotions or in depth feeling for anything in life-leave alone relationships. The boss was so manipulative on taking the credit for software prepared by his employees.

Nowadays we are living with luxurious life though we don't get peace to listen our own inner voice. This new generation is using advanced technology. Due to this drastic change in life, people live a life in distance and under disappointment, misery, tension etc. The solution to the problem of call center employees arrives in the form a motivational and soul searching advice from God that one should not blindly follow the Americans and that they can achieve happiness only if they follow their inner call which instigates and guides us in the right direction and that the four principles which create success are intelligence, imagination, self-confidence and to be really successful one must face failure and not remain snuggled in one's comfort zone. The fact is that money is not progress in building something lasting for the future.

Inter Relationship Sentiments

The expression of Indian nationalism is given even greater prominence in **One Night @ Call Center** because it is metaphorically connected to the central love interest in the novel, the narrative of Shyam's relationship with Priyanka. The changes of reconciliation are apparently imperiled by priyanka impending marriage to the NRI Ganesh, a Lexus-driving Microsoft employee in the United States. Priyanka is first happy when she is engaged to Ganesh Gupta, who works for Microsoft but becomes furious when she hears that her parents have planned her marriage the very next month, which she feels is too early. Both her mother and Ganesh press her to agree to this proposal. She is even more saddened by the fact that Shyam was eavesdropping on her conversation with Ganesh. When Vroom and Shyam show her that Ganesh had forged his pictures to hide his baldness, she disapproves Ganesh for having cheated her. Over the course of the novel, however, this relationship becomes a metonym for the relationship between Indian entrepreneurialism and the Indian economy, with India's marriage to foreign capital playing the role of the dishonest NRI. This extended imagery culminates in the mistaken identification of Microsoft's in-program testing code as a "bug" which proves that "nothing is perfect", even Microsoft Word (Bhagat 257). Shortly after, Ganesh is likewise shown to have feet of clay, when it is revealed that the photograph which he has been using to secure a bride has been retouched, with an unflattering bald spot removed.

Military Uncle tries to be nice to his son and grandson. But when he sends some pictures via mail to his grandson, his son loses his cool and asks him to keep out of his life. This leaves Military Uncle heartbroken. One has the strategic vision and managerial leadership and the like to do well in life. They were shallow with no emotions or in depth feeling for anything in life-leave alone relationships. The boss was so manipulative on taking the credit for software prepared by his employees.

Supernatural influence

Some circumstances issue in the novel ***One Night @ the Call Center***, The phone call from God is one of the salient features in the novel. The author has represented god as a friendly figure rather than a boss. He is shown as speaking in modern English rather than the stereo-typical pure English or Latin. All the lead characters of the novel decide to go and enjoy at a night club. After enjoying for a while, they leave for office. Midway through the journey, Vroom starts to feel revolted after drinking alcohol and so they stop and venture out. Vroom throws up and also breaks the window-pane of a shop thus spreading an alarm. They rush out of the place in fear. While frequent, they face a life-threatening situation when their Qualis crashes into a construction site hanging over a net of iron construction rods. As the rods began to yield slowly, they started to panic. They are unable to call for help as there is no mobile phone network at that place. In this situation, Shyam's mobile phone starts ringing.

The phone call is from God. He speaks to all of them and gives them suggestions to improve their life. After that, God also advises them on how to get their vehicle out of the construction site. The conversation with God motivates the group to such an extent that they get ready to face their problems with utmost determination and motivation. Meanwhile Vroom and Shyam hatch up a plan to throw Bakshi out of the call center and prevent the closing of Connexions call center, whose employees are to be downsized fundamentally. When they emerge out of danger, they have clear-cut goals in their mind. On returning to the Call Center, they carry out their plans with dexterity.

Conclusion

This paper has attempted to express multiple perspectives on the circumstes changes in technology using society as they affect in science fiction the secret of success for **ChetanBhagat.** He selects subject which a reader can associate with socio scientific issues. His language is very lucid and easy to understand. In this novel, ChetanBhagat reveals harsh truths about call centers, a dark part which can't be seen by anyone else. Even we can relate our life to any character in the novel. The entire novel is divided into two parts. All characters live mechanized lives. The novelist describes family issue, problems of work place etc. in a genuine and interesting way. The second part of the novel deals with reformation of all characters. **Chetan Bhagat** has segmented with a mix of sentiment, exploitations, romance, religion, supernatural influence, political conflict thoughts and family issue and technology and also social message depicted in the novel 'One night@ the call center'.

CHAPTER ELEVEN

Exposition of the contemporary Indian society in Chetan Bhagat's 'One night@ the call center': A study

This essay examines the way in which popular fiction had its impact upon **Chetan Bhagat** novels. As a well-known novelist he has created a firm place in the minds of the modern readers. He has portrayed young dynamic and modern Indian youth trying hard to become successful in their lives. He is gifted with an extraordinary ability to deal with various aspects of human life and also has keen interest in screenplays and spirituality. His characters represent middle class society and story seems real life story. The information declares that the author is not from literary background, still the story telling techniques used in his novel reveals his creative ability and love for art. It has been constant discussions about Bhagat's novels that which form of genre they should be kept in? Many of the views consider it as popular literature; Bhagat's novels are well thought-out as popular fictions. But at this juncture a question has been aroused that on what basis they can be counted popular?

Popular fiction aims at the entertainment of the people in mass. The popular fiction or kind of literature is written by simple and easy language. Bhagat is writing is also simple and clear. The novel is written in a comfortable natural style, without complicated and difficult words. By presenting the recent phenomena of day to day life of middle class people, he has kept behind a humorous classification to take pleasure in.

The popular fiction does not refer much philosophical or ideological issue. As it is explained, it is purely written for the sake of entertainment. It does not present deeper sense; instead it talks about the outer layer of human beings. If it presents philosophical or ideological issues, they are just to provide more pleasure and entertainment. The story talks about their messed up lives but in very simple manner. It presents the situation directly and not by using any kind of ambiguity.

This kind of work of art deals with popular tales or stories. They mostly rely on something said or discussed and something of that kind which presents issues of interest in general. **One night @ the call center** deals with the problems of people working in the call center, which are the recent issues of today's world as the youth by and large are fascinated by this kind of working system? Along with this, some part of the novel talks about different human relationships like mother and daughter relation through Priyanka and her mother's characters etc. It tries to present complexity with simplicity. It is said that the human being and their relations with each other are the most confusing aspect to understand. But here Bhagat has presented all confusing fact of humans in every simple way. It is a fine work of fiction. This novel is a short, well composed, has some fine comic sentences and most of all the whole novel is based on only one night. It is true that the story of one night may not contain so many points, subjects and thrills so the author includes some flash back memory of the hero. But for this technique it should be said that the author handled the situation with extreme brilliance. Bhagat's narrations are very simple as all the characters are introduced in the beginning only with very simple idea. The call center Qualis come to pick up all the employees every day at the home spot.

The story of six persons is working in a call center connexions in **Gurgaon** near **Delhi.** This center answers complains from the customers of an American home appliance company. The most suffering victim in **Shyam,** his boss wants him to do extra work along with his regular task, **"Bakshi** was sucking me into several hours outside my shift to teach new recruits" (44). Along with **Shyam** all the group members are unhappy with their manager **Mr.Bakshi.** Not only their job but they all are dissatisfied with their life as all have one or the other problem. They try to deal with problems with their own style, "Everyone wanted to get out of his or her miseries, if only for a few moments." The novel shows every aspect of life of these people.

Bakshi submits to website designed by **Shyam** and **Varun**to their U.S Company by saying it was his own creation. His girlfriend **Priyanka** has her own problems. Her mother has lots of problems with Priyanka and almost every day they have argument on one or the other issues, "Oh yes. She is the Miss Universe of melodrama. We cry together at least once a week."(95) Her mother wants her to select someone from settled NRI for marriage, but she was in love with Shyam but finally she gets ready to marry one NRI man found by his mother. **Radhika** is a mature girl, positive about her social life, but still her mother in law and her husband do not care for her at all, the message of her husband reveals it, "show elders respect. **Esha**wants to be a model; she has all the beauty but not enough height. She tried hard to get some modeling assignments, but nothing comes out in the name of action. **Varun** has problem with his father, and also with his job and boss. Military uncle wants to live with his son and family, but they don't consider him worthy enough to live with. Along with these personal problems they all have a new problem of losing their jobs, as it has been heard that to resize, company is going to fire some employees. These people are loaded with problems, but come in their life.

One night they go out for some relief. That was a different night. While returning back in hurry they take a short cut and meet with an accident. None of them hurt but the situatation was such where nobody knows what to do? And at that moment they get a phone call, even though there wasn't signal. It was not a regular call. It was a call from God.

God gives them all necessary solution to come to life again, they become able to save their life from that accident. When they reach again to the call center, they all have new energy, new ideas and new thinking, new vision towards life. With the help of God's suggestion, they all get a new life. Everyone meets a happy ending, not only characters but also readers. As it is clear the purpose of the popular fiction is to give pleasure, Bhagat also gives a happy ending, which gives enough entertainment to the readers.

Conclusion

The novel presents day-to-day life of people in general; it doesn't deal with hi-fi philosophical thoughts and issues. Along with problems, it focuses on more homesick feelings and unhappy moments, as a common person has. It is more interesting because the novel is centered on the contemporary world of India's new generation. Life is very complex, but Bhagat has presented it in a very simple way with easy language. It is a simple story, told in an interesting manner. Thus, using simple language Bhagat targets large number of readers, and has succeeded in that mission. Finally it turns out to be a peep into the new generation, their jobs, life, attitude, values and their dreams, thats makes the popular fiction "one night @ the call center".

CHAPTER TWELVE

Cross culture conflict in Chetan Bhagat's "2 states- the story of my marriage"

The central theme of paper goes about the cross cultural conflict in this novel "**2 states- the story of my marriage.** "Cross-cultural conflicts are no mystery to the inhabitants of the Indian subcontinent. It is an ever-present reality. ChetanBhagat's**"2 states -*the story of my marriage*"** deals with this issue. Partly autobiographical, the tale of two people belonging to two different states and communities is weaved together with instances from the author's own life. Their relationship traverses the stages of friendship, passion and love to the decision to get married, but they have to overcome the ultimate test, staunch opposition to their union from their respective parents whether their love proves strong enough to win over their families. The reluctance of people of different states to bridge cultural difference especially when it is an inter caste; inter community or interstate marriage in India. The author has excellently converted this accepted unfair reality into a perfect and full-fledged story and also the author's slightly wicked sense of humours underlying the narrative at various places serves to show real-life situations with genuineness and naturalness.

ChetanBhagat has been hailed as the most popular, important and biggest selling Indian author in English Language. India is well known for its varied cultural heritage as it is known for the lively and traditionally diverse marriages. '2 States' is a story of a marriage which is as simple as it can get, yet so complicated. Chetan Bhargat's novel concentrates on how a particular phenomenon, the concept of love relates to matters to ideology, race, social class and gender. It also concentrates in terms of social, political and economic situation. The novel 2 states deals with the cross-cultural conflict complimenting the different experiences and imbibing them meaningfully. As a rose symbolizes beauty, as a soldier symbolizes nation, the title of any work should symbolizes the theme. Chetan bhagat's 2 states-the title by itself showcases the association point of the two states coming into union. A simple but realistic novel, brilliantly explores the encounter of two states; Punjab and Tamil nadu. The two main characters cut their umbilical cord to get affixed with a new cord; the marital cord. With the merger of two souls in the name of love, there is a blending of two cultures, religions, languages, tradition and practices. Thus the two major characters shed their umbilical cord- their affectionate identity-and require a new identity.

Out of the several methods of marriage, two are predominant namely arranged marriage and love marriage. Basically, the love between a boy and girl leads to love marriage and generally and simply they take this decision. In the current scenario, the instances of love marriage are increasing, but these differ from country to country. But multiplicity of languages, castes and classes in India, the scenario is little different. The boy's family should love the girl and the girl's family should love the boy. Also boy's family should love the girl's family and the girl's family should love the boy's family. If in the meantime, the love between the girl and the boy continues, they get married with the blessings of the two families and live happily thereafter. In India arranged marriages are more common. In a situation of love between two persons that too from different states, communities or languages, the two parents and families do not generally agree. In some cases the lovers rebel, elope or perform court marriage without the consent / presence of their parents or even commit suicide. A better method is to try and convince the two families, even if it takes some time. (This novel by ChetanBhagat is said to be the real story of his own marriage, although many names etc.)

It has anecdotes from his life; a reflection of his marriage to a South Indian Brahmin. Since the book is drawn from his life experiences, it makes for an interesting book to read. This novel revolves around **Krish** and **Ananya;** hailing from two different states in India and their simple love story laced with details as they decide to take the thrust. The families do not approve of the various traditions and think low of the future of their marital harmony. This novel is a take on inter-religious marriages and their assumed ambiguity in India. ‘2 States’ by ChetanBhagat takes you on a splendid journey to the land of mystic splendor India. A boy from Punjab falls in love with a girl from Tamil Nadu and they decide to tie the knot. This novel is about an IIMA couple’s struggle to marry over the cultural differences. Krish is north Indian Punjabi boy in love with Tamilian Brahmin girl Ananya. The only catch is, Krish and Ananya don’t want to elope or be estranged to their families, and therefore, they choose to convince their parents for the marriage.

Both Ananya and Krish take turns to win over each other’s families like each other. In fact, Krish does get 4 gold rings made to purpose girl’s entire family! Though the idea is most realistic, it draws ones attention to cultural differences in various India. In India cross cultural marriages are still looked upon critically let alone an inter-state marriage. Added to that Punjabis are clearly different from Tamilians; Punjabis are well known for their disorder, richness and easy attitude while Tamilians for their good manners and uncommunicativeness. However, the couple in question is exceptions and much in love. They choose the difficult path of winning over the hearts of their parents and seek their blessings instead of eloping.

They try and make this work by Krish getting a job at Citibank Chennai, Ananya's hometown where she's working in HLL and pays visits to her house to warm up to her parents and brother. Ananya does her part by making a short trip to Delhi, Krish's hometown to meet his mother. The story recounts what all they do to make odds meet and whether they succeed or not.Bhagat manages to provide an interesting perspective to a common problem faced by youngsters today, familial opposition when marrying out of community and interstate. The reluctance of people of different states to bridge cultural differences language and religious etc. "Cultures change for sure, but the shift in people's thinking, outlook and worldview is gradual. Culture isn't just our food, arts and traditions in a broader sense, culture defines it, who are as people, how aim to live their lives, what acceptable or unacceptable behavior and who in society is rewarded and punished. Most important, our culture contains the implicit rules by which we live – our values"Bhagat has a more difficult time describing values within Indian culture" When think of Indian values, we normally think of personal values – such as family, religion and respect for elders. These things are notably Indian. The intention of the novel is good. It wants to bring out the racial prejudices that still exist among people belonging to different states and more evident as North-South divide.

There are two ways to look at the racial comments and humour in this novel. Punjabi characters making racial comments about South Indians, may be this what happened in his real life and author wanted to be true to the characters Even Krish making some observations about Tamil culture and habits is bit understandable: Punjabi boy landing in Chennai for first time and getting bothered with new people around him.

Form the puzzle to the prologue which passionately tells, this is all about how two communities face difficulties to understand each other and when one start to realize half way through, that it is going to end like this and as the fan inside one feels sad as to why resort to formula for preaching people that should unite as a nation to great extent, that **Krish**himself makes fun of the line that need love only for the sake of uniting the nation, he springs up a surprise when **Anaya's** father says that it was not a community, it was like that how to behave with the people around us. When**Krish** started to tell his mother about **Ananya**, his mother gets angry besides her busy work of cutting vegetables. Unfortunately the knife hits his mother's finger and she tossed of pain and says: "kill me. Kill me for this girl (38). Like that there are many incidents that take place in the novel. The couples in question are exceptions and much in love. They choose the difficult path of winning over the hearts of their parents and seek their blessings instead of eloping.

The novel is first in its content which attempts to unite not only two states but also their traditions and cultures. It endeavors to represent the people of the nation only as Indians not as castes, religious, states etc. This is the only thing the novelist wants to carry to the youth of his country. With Krish and Ananya hailing from two different regions matters only take to worse. This novel delicately puts across these obvious differences in mindsets. The mismatch in the mental frameworks is absolutely, the way he brings in the differences and takes potshots at each other's cultural differences is bone tickling. Though the basis is most realistic, it draws your attention to cultural differences in diverse India.

Conclusion

Bhagat manages to provide an interesting perspective to a common problem faced by youngsters today, familial opposition when marrying out of community and interstate. The reluctance of people of different states to bridge cultural differences. ***Two States***is a refreshing love story that captures the sentiments and traditions etc in cross-culture marriages. Based on his real life experience, the story captures the love story of a typical Punjabi boy and a Tamil girl who not only convince each other about their marriage but their respective families as well. In India cross cultural marriages are still looked upon critically let alone an inter-state marriage. So, lastly the novel 2 states are highly appealing and tell the originality of the Indian society and its culture and tradition which is far more different than the western lifestyle and Marriage system.

CHAPTER THIRTEEN

A post-colonial perspective in Chetan Bhagat's "the three mistakes of my life"

This essay examines the way in which post-colonial perspectives impacting upon ChetanBhagat novels. He a well-known novelist has created a firm place in the minds of the modern readers. He has portrayed young dynamic and modern Indian youth trying hard to become successful in their lives. He comments upon the ethos in modern life. The issues that one feels one's own is reflected into his writing. Urban environment in his main concern. His characters represent middle class society. The story seems real life story and it unravels the minds of the contemporary youth especially when one refers to that is reflected in **The Three Mistakes of My Life**. It is very much contemporary India, easily relatable and identifiable to post-colonial perspective by the urban youth. Though India is no longer a colony but centuries of colonization have left some imprints of colonialism evident even in our country in the absence of the imperial power is a postcolonial perspective.

Colonial Theory

The novel **The Three Mistakes of My Life** is the post-colonial context, it is essential to keep in mind **Frantz Fanon's Three Stages** which the literature of the colonized passes through, "the first is a stage of assimilation, when the colonized, bewitched by the colonizers claim to cultural superiority, imitate their literature and plead for acceptance as cultural equals. Second is the stage when, dissatisfied with integration into culture of their contemptuous colonizers, they return to their old cultural roots. In the third stage they fashion a new and genuinely national culture, shaped loyalty to their rediscovered national identity [The Wretched of the Earth p.?]".

In this context, **Bhagat** has given **The Three Mistakes of My Life** from nationalistic motives. He has raised certain national issues like communal riots, religious bias, misguiding the youth by politicians and patriotism. Ali is made symbolic of Nationalism. Ali's loyalty comes to light in his preference for India even at the temptation of comforts and luxuries in Australia. Post colonialism can also be understood through power relations between the native people and the whites. The term is used, "to cover all the culture affected by colonial process from the moment of colonization to the present day. This is because there is a continuity of preoccupations throughout the historical process initiated by colonial aggregation [The Empire Writes Back, 1-2]". It is true in the context of Bhagat's novel too. Even after the fall down of the British Empire the domination of the whites continues most prominently the American call centers dominate India. As seen in **One Night @ Call Center**, the Indians at call centers work all night for their white masters on the other side of the globe.Bill Gate's **Microsoft** has given a new avatar to the third countries especially India. Now these computers have colonized an Indian people. The preliminary part of **The Three Mistakes of My Life** begins with Bhagat's opening of e-mail account. Govind alias the businessman sends a suicide note to Bhagat via Email. All this reveal that computers have become an expected part of the young generation and it is in tight grip of its stern masters i.e. the computers

The novel begins with a cricket match. There is a short view of the contemporary cricket players of the country as watched in one day international match of India vs Australia. The three friends spend the day in a lazy way watching cricket on T.V. Cricket fever is so communicable that even the shopkeepers in the market place could be seen celebrating victory of India. Realizing the dearth of sports shop in the area the three unemployed friends plan to open a cricket shop, "since cricket is the most popular game in Belrampur" [?].

Ambition is the quality of the colonizer. It is the ambition to rule which is instrumental ruling India for more than a four hundred years by the East India Company. Govind too harbors intense ambitiousness. Having the qualities of a businessman he wishes to own a shop in a mall. "Our shop has been doing good business but we can't grow unless we move to a new city location" (Bhagat 25). He diversifies the business and runs a stationary shop as well as starting Math's tuition and cricket coaching simultaneously.

The three friends belong to the native intellectual class whom Macaulay wanted to create among the Indians, Indian in blood and color, but English in taste, in opinion, in morals, and in intellect". Preference for branded wear is evident as Govind wears fake Reebok slippers. The three friends celebrate parties in the western way by opening a bottle of beer. They address each other stylishly as 'dude'. they have no inhibitions in using words like 'fuck' which are a forbidden in the native Indian context .like the call center employees in **one night @ the call center,** Bhagat has created youth who belong to the new generation preferring the anglicized culture of the west in the form of dress , mobiles, pizzas, beer, watching T.V and girls etc.

Though the Britons have receded back to its shores but seeds of the British policy of dividing and ruling have ruined so deep that it continues to develop and presents the contemporary political situation of India where the **BJP and Congress** are the two dominating political parties always at loggerheads the three friends visit Parekhji's residence at Bittoo mama's invitation: "The BJP gathering looked like a marriage party where only priests were invited. Most of them carried some from of ornament like a trishual or a rudraksha or a holy book [?]". Parikhji, a firm core politicians tries to draw in the three friends in the BJP fold by narrating incidents of violence faced by poor Hindus, but the Macaulay group do not have an influential mind on seeing, Ali's Father in the party conspicuous for his Muslim beard some party men called him Ali Baba and shouted, "get lost, your traitor".

Fanon points out, "there is a fact: white men consider themselves superior to black men. There is another fact: black men want to prove to white men, at all costs, the richness of their intellect ...."[Black Skin, White Masks10]. In this context Fred is the white man and the three friends with Ali are the black men. Fred quietly uses Australian slings like burl, piece of piss, full a wallop, mozzies, coldies, to draw off the python and the three friends not only try to learn these slangs but also use them after coming back to India. Govind calls mosquitoes as mozzies at Vidhya's house. There is a sense of superiority in Fred's behaviour as revealed from his conduct. He does not let Ali bowl on the first day in order to break his pride. He is proud of Australian players and says, "We love to dominate opponents but also love a fight. When there's a challenge it brings out the best" (Bhagat 161). When, he tells Govind that he is doing boring coach talk with Ish, "Ish's chest swelled with pride as Fred had called him equal in role" (Bhagat 161). Again there is a sense of superiority when Fred says, 'you want to know why Australia always wins" (Bhagat 161). Fred's eyes lighted up as he said that the AIS gave generous scholarships and best facilities to the players. Ish tries to equate with the circumstances and says, "imagine what would happen if we could have this kind of training in India" (Bhagat 163).Fanon describes the "assimilations phase" as "the native intellectual gives proof that he has assimilated the culture of the occupying power" (The Post-Colonial Studies Reader, 158). At the restaurant with the Australians the three friends enjoy NCR (Number of cans required) jokes on girls. Michael asks Omi to eat more proteins to which Omi replies that he guzzles two liters of milk every day.

A **Favonian** reading can be applied to women characters i.e. Govind's mother and Vidya. Fanon writes, "Face to face with this man who is 'different from himself', he needs to defend himself. Here Govind's mother is mistreated by two others i.e. the husband and the society as a woman in the Indian context has to play a role of subordination. Though the women have been domesticated and bound to servitude but lately there have been paradigm shifts. The new generation women have been taking bold steps. The role of women has become modern from traditional. Since Vidya transgress the acceptable boundaries of friendship with Govind. She was kept, "under house arrest. He had slammed her mobile phone to pieces" (Bhagat, 251). Vidya suffers because she is a woman but this kind of suffering is not faced by Govind. **Spivak** says, "...the ideological construction of gender keeps the male dominant. If, in the context of colonial production, the subaltern has no history and cannot speak, the subaltern as female in even more deeply in shadow"(Post colonialism, 1446).

The boldness on the part of the negro/Vidya threatens the presence of the dominant/parents/family/society. Through dominance and power the superior inflicts violence on the inferior. Vidya was confined to her room & later sent out of Ahmedabad. Govind's not responding to her SMSs must have left her heartbroken. Vidya invites this kind of treatment for her display of boldness by committing something forbidden by unmarried girl in India. Though India is no longer a colony but centuries of colonization have left some imprints of colonialism evident even in the absence of the Imperial power. Bhagat's '**The Three Mistakes of My Life**' is a postcolonial perspective is a fruitful exercise.

Conclusion

Chetan Bhagat is one of the most popular contemporary Indian novelists in English. He has portrayed young dynamic and modern Indian youth trying hard to become successful in their lives. He comments upon the ethos in modern life. He is gifted with an extraordinary ability to deal with various aspects of human life. His popularity as a writer rests basically on his intimate understanding of human nature. He is an outstanding writer who concentrates emotional harmony of the third generation of India and ambition of the youth which is mixed with fears and also his novel gone through a lot of transformation from its initial days to the present times and has attained a whole new intensity in terms of concept passion of people, business and impact upon apost-colonial perspective. Though India is no longer a colony but centuries of colonization have left some marks of colonialism evident even in the absence of the colonial power.

CHAPTER FOURTEEN

Various cultural issues on Chetan Bhagat selected novels: A study

This essay focuses on different culture issues in chetan Bhagat's selected novels. He is one of the most popular contemporary Indian novelists in Indian English Literature. He has portrayed young dynamic and modern Indian youth culture, trying hard making them successful in their lives. He is gifted with an extraordinary ability to deal with various aspects of human life. His popularity as a writer is basically on his intimate understanding of human nature in different perspectives. ChetanBhagat novel deals with different culture perspectives from culture issues and has raised certain culture issues like communal riots, religion, bias, misguiding the youth by politician etc. He brings about corporate culture is a term used to describe beliefs and a value system that provides its unique taste and attitude to a friendship in Cosmo-culture, the condition of youth is very pathetic. In this world of Cosmo-culture, everybody is involved in an extra marital relationship etc. In his novel "*One Night @ the Call Center* bring is modern culture in India. Today in India youngster may keep unsocial hours, neglect his family obligations, drink excessive cocktails and date each other with a casualness that horrifies parents. Everybody wants high salary, fashionable life style. The call center is only a representative place of modern India. The youth is teased by the modern culture and facilities. They are our country's most productive western culture .Chetan Bhagat brings interreligious marriage in India is well known for its varied cultural heritage as it is known for the lively and traditionally various marriage *"2 States the story of my marriage"* Though the idea is most realistic modern trend, it draws attention to cultural differences in diverse India. . India requires a deep understanding of culture and diversely of mankind religious and languages.

Definition of culture

Culture is the characteristics and knowledge of a particular group of people, defined by everything from language, religion, cuisine, social habits, music and arts. (Or) culture is a way of life of a group of people--the behaviors, beliefs, values, and symbols that they accept, generally without thinking about them, and that are passed along by communication and imitation from one generation to the next.

The Center for Advance Research on Language Acquisition goes a step further, defining culture as shared patterns of behaviors and interactions, cognitive constructs and understanding that are learned by socialization. Thus, it can be seen as the growth of a group identity fostered by social patterns unique to the group. The word "culture" derives from a French term, which in turn derives from the Latin "colere," which means to tend to the earth and grow, or cultivation and nurture. "It shares its etymology with a number of other words related to actively fostering growth," *Cristina De Rossi*, an anthropologist at Barnet and Southgate College in London, told Live Science.

"Many countries are largely populated by immigrants, and the culture is influenced by the many groups of people that now make up the country. This is also a part of growth. As the countries grow, so does its cultural diversity".

Multiculturalism

The concept of global culture once again has voted for the celebration of all cultures that different from country to country or region to region but on worldwide level, they contribute to one global culture. When one talks of country, the concept of Indian culture arises. However, when one talks of global culture, the concept of Indian culture gives put to culture of India. Again, it is much more that. Adaptation and synthesis are two virtues that make alive in spite of many races, tribes, languages, religions and creeds. Cultural synthesis is in her blood. Spirituality is life-breath. Yoga is strength. The figure of the cosmic dance of Shiva is her symbol that reveals the concept of creation, preservation and destruction. Though the Western culture has embraced her body closely, spirit remains untouched. The concept of compound culture is yielding place to the light of multiculturalism that values the uniqueness of different cultures and traditions. The western storm, no doubt, has shaken the leaves of Indian culture but failed to destroy its roots that are firm and strong in their spiritual foundation. The spirit of tolerance and cosmopolitanism already includes the concept of multiculturalism in itself. (K.Arora Sudhir-2012)

We are living in age of liberalization and globalization. The ideology that is used primarily in the discourse of economics has come to dominate the discourse of all the social sciences as well as the general social discourse. All these ideologies are so much tangle come together that it is almost impossible to think of them one by one and for the present purpose. The globalization used to represent all of this together and mostly talking, globalization stand for open rivalry in market, liberal strategy and free business etc. It has resulted in model of life that never seen or experienced during earlier times in human history. Metropolitan cities, information technology, fast food, immigration, customaries, free industry etc. are a few of the noticeable forms of life. Fresh air and open area gives migraine and Malls and multiplexes give a new rent of life. The object has definitely changed. This event has huge implications. First, and foremost, the center of the essentially hierarchical structure lies with the West and establishes the superiority of Western things like advanced technology, money, cutthroat competition, nuclear families, success at any rate etc. It sidelines eastern concepts like joint families, speed-slow life, mutual reliance, spirituality etc., It is impact, by consumes other cultural patterns, promotes one culture and kills plurality. Everything is reduced to pay-packages, hotel living, be able to MNC food, quick technological changes and fast changing paradigms. In short, it causes cultural changes. Though it claims to free from chain up of narrow-mindedness, it seems to be working against multiplicity and Multiculturalism.

A multicultural society is one that continually develops and is making stronger by the contribution of it is a variety of peoples. This perspective also make possible not only to recognize structural and hierarchal relationships of different constituent cultural groups of a better culture but also the need to resolve such differences and helps develop the strategies required to resolve, definitely not to dissolve, the differences. Globalization gives an opposite impetus to the society by spread multiculturalism. Human being societies, by their very nature, tend to have differences, so anything that facilitates demolition of differences, even with the willful cooperation of the people, and howsoever ideal or ideologically correct it might be projected, may not essentially be favourable to the growth of humanity. Multiplicity of all kinds-lingual, social, traditional-being at possibility- must be protected in all ways of life. (Ms.Renu Singh and Ms. Shikha-2013)

Modern culture issues in chetanbhagat novels

The culture of modern India has evolved many folds since the ancient ages. The history of India has played a significant role in shaping up the Indian culture. In the historical past, India has been invaded several times and this brought in a mix of cultures. The other factors that contributed towards shaping the culture of India are its unique geography and different religions. The modern Indian culture is more evolved version of the ancient cultures in India. Also the modern Indian culture has been profoundly in influenced by the western culture. Post-independence the culture of India began to evolve further to what is the call the modern Indian culture. There can be clearly in its architecture, performing arts, food, clothing and festivals etc "Cultures are not a matter of being but of becoming" (Babba). There are no cultures that comes together leading to hybrid forms instead cultures are the consequences of attempts to still the flux of culture hybirdity. Therefore cultures come after the hybridizing process rather than existence of culture.

Chetan Bhagat's novel **"One Night @ the Call Center"** in this novel revolves around a group of six call center employees working in Connexions call center in Gurgaon, Haryana. It takes place during the span of one night, in which all of the leading characters confront some aspect of themselves or their lives they would like to change. The story takes a dramatic and decisive turn through literal dues ex- machine, when the characters get a phone call from God."

Chetan Bhagat **brings** modern culture in India. The themes involve the anxieties and insecurities of the rising Indian middle class, including questions about career, inadequacy, marriage, family conflicts in a changing India, and the relationship of the young Indian middle class to both executives and ordinary clients whom they serve in the U.S.A. It's the story of a group of people working at a call center. All of them have personal problems in life, however, they are friends rather colleagues working together. Their call center is under the threat of closure because of the economic slowdown and other reasons. 'They are our country's most productive western culture'. It is true in the context of Bhagat's novel too. Even after the fall down of the British Empire the domination of the Whiteman continues most prominently the American call centers dominate India. As seen in **One Night @ Call Center**, the Indians at call centers work all night for their white masters on the other side of the globe.Bill Gate's **Microsoft** has given a new avatar to the third countries especially India. Now these computers have colonized an Indian people .Chetan Bhagat narrates the episode of 'God' when all characters are at climax when they are near to death. The characters apparently listen to their inner voice and suggest them the way on that they are moving irresponsible and not successful. There is no network but there is a call from God and after that there is a radical change in everybody's life.

ChetanBhagat brings about corporate culture is a term used to describe beliefs and a value system that provides its unique taste and attitude of friendship in Cosmo-culture in which the condition of youth is very pathetic. In this world of Cosmo-culture, everybody is involved in an extra marital relationship etc. The novel chosen for the assessment is **One Night @ the Call Center** in this the author has portrayed the modern culture in India. Today in India youngster may keep unsocial hours, neglect his family obligations, drinks excessive, has cocktails and date each other with a casualness that horrifies parents. Everybody wants high salary, fashionable life style. The call center is only a representative place of modern culture in India. The youth is teased by the modern culture and facilities...**ChetanBhagat** brings interreligious marriage in India is well known for its varied cultural heritage as it is known for the lively and traditionally various marriages in his novel **'2 States the story of my marriage'.** Though the idea is most realistic modern trend, it draws attention to cultural differences in diverse India. . India requires a deep understanding of culture and diversely of mankind religious and languages. It's mythical, supernatural often contradicting, yet fascinating journey through western culture.

As the fast rising technology has invaded our lives together with the vast social networking, there have been several new words which have been commonly used. Most of them are abbreviations that, only those who are inclined to the latest trends can understand. Now a day's young writers are turned up with the new technical and Indianite words which are becoming substitute for literal words to which one may say, it's a new dawn of words. These words are reflections of contemporary progress of computer science and technology and of various cultures along with the medium and medium of educations. These words don't have any literal glimpses but are fitted wonderfully to literal words. Youngsters are common users of these words, showing cut of changing languages. As Youngsters are more prone with new technology and variety of regional cultures, evolution of language is marginalized with technical elevation along with mulifacets of language.

His novel **"2 States: The Story of My Marriage"** commonly known as it is the story about a couple coming from two different states in India, who face hardships in convincing their parents to approve of their marriage. The novel is said to be inspired from the real life story of the author and his wife AnushaSuryaNarayanan who are from Delhi and Tamil Nadu, respectively." It is true in the context of Bhagat's novels.

He brings interreligious marriage in India is well known for its varied cultural heritage as it is known for the lively and traditionally diverse marriage **'2 States the story of my marriage'** which as simple as it can get, yet so elaborate. It is a well-known fact the marriages in India are more of a family affair where the brides and the grooms' families approve of one another before the couples tie the knot. '2 **States the Story of My Marriage'** about an IIM couple's struggle to marry over the different cultureless. They get married. Welcome to 2 States, a story about Krish and Ananya. They are from two different states of India, deeply in love and want to get married. Of course, their parents don't agree. To convert their love story into a love marriage, the couple has a tough battle in front of them.

Krish in **2 States the Story of My Marriage** is north Indian Punjabi boy in love with Tamil Brahmin girl Ananya. (ChetanBhagat too is Punjabi and his wife is a South Indian.) The only catch is, Krish and Ananya don't want to elope or be separated to their families, and therefore, they choose to convince their parents for the marriage. Both Ananya and Krish take turns to win over each other's families and then they try to make both the families like each other. After all in India, one does not marry the guy or girl of his or her choice. Though the idea is most realistic in modern trend, it draws one's attention to cultural differences in diverse India.

The story revolves around Krish and Ananya - hailing from two different states in India and their simple love story laced with details as they decide to take the plunge. The families do not approve of the diverse traditions and think low of the future of their marital harmony. The book is a take one inter-religious marriages and their alleged ambiguity in modern Indian culture.

ChetanBhagat says in India, when a boy and girl love each other there is a sequence of events that arise before the marriage. The family needs to approve of the each other and the events that proceed are fodder for drama, verbal arguments etc. Love marriages in India are often a bumpy ride with arranged marriage being the families' preference parent's opinion does matter to youngsters and Bhagat is one of those to whom it matters a great deal with modern Indian culture.

Chetan Bhagat's novels touch an emotional chord of the modern generation of India. His metro-novel displays the ambition of the youth which is mixed with fears and tinged with tears. His men and women are stayed from morality and their only motto in life is – eat, drink, and enjoy life. Behind their happiness existential trouble is hidden about their future and unrelenting presence of their past. This admixture of humour, pathos, hopes and fears and success and failure brands his work of modern generation India. Two generations after independence, one of the essential characteristics of the new India is that the educated middle class who once turned to English for business applications now see it in a different culture.

Socio culture values

India is a multi-cultural and multi-religious society. Culture describes the many ways in which human beings express themselves for the purposes of uniting with others, forming a group, defining an identity, and even for distinguishing themselves as unique. Values have a moral and regulatory role and have a wider significance in going beyond specific situations. For example, Chetan Bhagat's novel, 'The 3 mistakes of my life' Post-Godhra riots put all the protagonists into a dangerous situation where Govind and Ishaan lose their loved friend Omi. However, they are successful in saving the life of Ali, which was a major challenge at the time of crisis. The Indian society is not a huge one. This is a natural effect to the fact that diversity is a part of the Indian way of life. From region to region, variety in the social structure outstandingly seen. Unity in variety is best seen in India in a maze of seemingly different peoples. One social unifier is the Indian system of caste adhered to by all the racial groups belonging to the Hindu religion. Moreover, socialism, passion also plays their destructive part in India's socio-cultural life.

Human values are most definitely different from moral values. Moral values regard matters of right and wrong, human values are shifty things, often confused with morals. They change from person to person, from day to day and hour to hour, into whatever currently suits people. Human values, while occasionally in friendship with moral values, are usually things that benefit the group of people, or person, pursuing them. In the last section of the book, the author has portrayed the incident in a very realistic manner that by saving a Muslim the protagonists convert themselves as human beings. It was so much a matter of pride that they have such people among their who do not care about the community and the religions but feelings make them the real heroes of life. On the other hand, there are some party workers in the novel who are ready to kill Ali but after Govind offer them money; they are ready to leave the boy, Ali. Man can do anything to get money. Through the life of Govind, ChetanBhagat wants to maybe show that if they are disciplined, considerate and not irritation they might lead a successful life. In our society, some people live with lot of dreams and desires. They are also ready to face any disaster to satisfy their ego and to get more respect in the society.

Socialism has played a key role in shaping the religious history of modern India. The 1947 partition of India bring about rebellion among Hindus, Muslims, and Sikhs in Punjab, Bengal, Delhi, and other parts of India; Five lakh people died as a result of the violence. Since its independence, India has periodically witnessed large-scale violence sparked by underlying tensions between sections of its majority Hindu and minority Muslim communities. A well-known allegation that Indian political parties make against their rivals is that they play vote bank politics, and give political support to issues for the single purpose of gaining the votes of the members of a particular community. Caste-based politics is also important in India; caste-based discrimination and the reservation system continue to be major issues that emotionally debated. Many of Ahmedabad's buildings were set on fire by Hindu and Muslim mobs during the 2002 Gujarat violence that the author has illustrated. There are people of our country who cannot come out of their social boundaries. For example, in the Godhra Incident of the novel Bitoo mama is adamant in take revenge the death of his own son and other Hindus. He and his party workers burn Muslims to take revenge.

The Indian society is even today an agglomeration of numerous castes, tribes and religious communities. Castes are systems of occupation, endogamy, social culture, social class, political power the assignment of individual to places in the social hierarchy is determined by social group and cultural heritage. The caste identity has become a subject of political, social and legal interpretation. Communities who are getting, listed as entitled for positive discrimination do not get out of this list even if their social and political conditions get better. In many cases, the legal system is involved to decide if a certain person is entitled for positive discrimination. However, with all this positive discrimination policy, most of the communities who were low in the caste hierarchy remain low in the social order even today. Moreover, communities who were high in the social hierarchy remain even today high in the social hierarchy. Indian society has divided since ancient times into several thousands of groups, castes or communities called 'Jāti'. In spite of the present day use of the same phrase to describe both 'Varna and Jāti', some observers have claimed that the caste system is ideological rather than religiously motivated, for example K. Srinivasulu claims: The *Varna* system is of no significance to an understanding of the present day caste situation except in broad ideological terms. Any attempt to examine the caste system by fitting it into the classical *Varna* model would be of limited relevance in understanding its role in the socio-political processes of contemporary India.Fanaticism refers to excessive extremism of opposing views. Religious fanaticism has shown to be correlated with orthodoxy and the self-importance given by an individual to himself. It is connected with consciousness, location and community. Religious fanaticism is a growing global problem that has crippled almost every nation in the world. It demands a great sense of awareness and awakening from humanity to grow out of this attitude.

Those who are power hungry and misuse their influences and power use the concept of religious extremism. The rural mass is still backward in our country because of fanaticism. Fanaticism makes them orthodox largely so that it becomes difficult to uplift them in any respect. As long as the world does not cultivate a sense of mutual respect, tolerance for the other violence will never come to end. They may say that this happens only because of the decline in socio-cultural and religious declines in India. The novelist shows a positive way out to this situation by depicting people like Govind, Ishaan and Omi understand the real value of life and intend to do well for India. They walk on the right track. But sometimes circumstances are unfavourable which bring irritation. These circumstances are of politics and this politically fragmented culture makes it very difficult to take any decisive action. Therefore, people sometimes remain inactive and become victims of evil activities. When there is no way for the suffering people, they revolt against this evil system. Our social-cultural values are like waves that sometimes remain reasonably stable but sometimes turn and twist the entire system. That means the morality of the inner state of mind is never destroyed towards the end of life, but in front of the materialistic world people rapidly change their decision. They can say that it arouses more greed for earning money or wealth. To some extent, their great expectations become the reason for murder, suicide etc. Therefore, these issues co-related with each other and connected with the orthodox society. And the coming generation is trying to bring change in it that is a matter of pride for all of us. It is commonplace to say that nation's future lies in its youth. But the future of India also lies in its youthfulness. Bhagat focuses on one specific issue to expose the radical changes taking place in the postmodern society where fragmentation has become the keynote of life. (.Anjana Prajapati-2013)

Paradoxical symbol of Cultural corner

The paradoxical symbol of cultural corner of both Panjabi's and Tamils from the within and without the communities keeps the novel from being unfair one way or the other. The earlier perception of both the communities to view each other in hierarchal terms changes to adopting an ideologically more correct position of acceptance and appreciation of difference and also an effort to not to make any effort to dissolve the difference can be taken to be reflective of a multicultural point of view. Krish and Ananya are individuals as well as types and represent a community, howsoever little it may be—that is highly educated and refuse to accept the neo-colonialism at various levels. In this era, they represent the state of affairs where some of such people start remembers their ethnicity without losing their modern western English speaking administrative class status. Postcolonial theory is indeed a very complex theory constituting numerous paradigms within it. One of the paradigms used in this novel is the assertion of native culture. Krish and Ananya get married having won over their respective parents and parents-in-law. The way their families come forward, though they have different cultural background, or respect the cultural differences are significant, positive and healthy sign of a progressive society. The younger generation of India subscribes to this new value system without any feelings of grief.

Bhagat's novel *2 States* read by these younger people tries to attain a balance between these opposite positions. The story supports the new pattern of life not by propagating a 'to hell with you oldies' but by propagating a first taking that extra step which is required in all bridging situation. Bhagat, thus makes an effort to reconcile the tensions of contemporary life rather than evenly accusing either of them. It is for this that the novelist may be hail than brushed off for writing in the popular mode and adopting an easy, almost sentimental, text-book type attitude towards the serious cultural issues. (Ms.Reu Singh and Ms. Shikha-2013)

BPO Culture

ChetanBhagat in his second novel, *one night @ the call center*, attempts to cover the life of a new generation of youth that has emerged since the establishment of BPOs in the country. The book exposes the reality of the modern era of call centers. Call centers or business process have taken over the country in the extent of the last few years. The call centers serve mostly the UK and US.Call centers can be seen to have helped India develop. Almost 70% of its youth today are employed in call centers. They serve as mass recruitment organizations. As a fresher, one could start his career in an International Call Center as a call center Executive and earn highly attractive pay packages. The wide range of opportunities, there are comparatively well paid jobs for minimum qualification and the facilities the companies provide like to and fro transport, subsidized meals and medical facilities makes call centers a good option. (Anjuri)

The call center job may seem easy for others but it requires wonderful amount of hard work and the Indian youth are willing to perform. The only requirement to work in a call center is good command over English. Youngsters who are not so fluent in the language also go through training and start their jobs.

Shyam, the narrator of the story is also the leader of the group. He breaks up with his girl friendPriyanka and has to face the consequent struggles. He does not know how to assert himself against his boss Bakshi, who does not understand the pressures he is facing. His friend Varun, also called Vroom, is passionate about fast a bike that explains his nickname. Priyanka, Shyam'sex girlfriend cannot make up her mind as to whether she should be free to go after what she wants and please her mother. After the breakup she has the prospect of marrying a rich NRI guy. Esha is a modern girl. She is also a model hopeful who belongs to a small town. She is so independent that she comes out of her house without her parents' consent to become a model. Radhika is a married woman who lives with her mother-in-law, while her husband Anuj works in Kolkata. The Military Uncle always found lonely and divided throughout the novel.

The life of youth in call centers is about 'management,' acquiring required skill set,' 'and becoming go-getters.' (*One night @ the call center* -13) Most of the young people working in call centers have no social life outside the office. Their friends are either colleagues in their call center or other call centers. Esha says, 'I hardly have any friends outside the WASG.'(*One night @ the call center*, 60) In India, most of the social engagements are around dinner. Therefore, they miss out such opportunities because of their working hours at night. The employees have no choice and no time to spend with their family and relatives. Shyam does not find time to attend even his cousin or neighbors' marriage.

Love for money is predominantly found among the present day youth. Vroom feels that, 'there is activism in chasing money.' (*One night @ the call center* 47) All the call center employees struggle night after night so that they can have some money with which they can fulfil their simple dreams. Priyanka comes to work in the call center to earn enough money to do her B.Ed., and to build a nursery school.

The general feeling of call center employees is that Americans are successful because of their money power. Even Vroom in *One Night @ The Call Center* feels that "the only reason Americans have a say in this world is because they have cash. The day we get money, we can screw them. So, the first thing we have to do is get the money." (One *night @ the call center* 48) He also feels that the Americans act superior to them only because of their monetary power.

'Why do some fat-ass, dim-witted Americans get to act superior to us? Do you know why?'

Nobody answered.

Vroom continued, 'I'll tell you why. Not because they are smarter. Not because they are better people. But because their country is rich and ours is poor.' (*One night @ the call center* 119)

Priyanka's mother wants her daughter to get married to a well settled person in spite of knowing that her daughter is in love with the call center agent Shyam. She considers Shyam a 'loser' as he does not earn more like Ganesh to whom she is eager to marry off Priyanka. She wants Priyanka to marry Ganesh because he is rich and gets a predictable cash flow at the end of every month. She also feels Ganesh to be a good, well-settled match for her daughter. Shyam comments on this attitude among most Indians.

Vroom is the representative of a modern stylish youth. He loves jeans, pizzas, mobiles, bikes and partying with girls. His parents are divorced and the reason he works at the call center is to get a good salary that would help him keep up with his lavish life-style. He says, "It will suck if I lose my fifteen grand a month. If I don't get my pizza thrice a week, I will die." (*One night @ the call center*, 95)After all bikes, pizzas and cell phones come only at a cost. But at heart he dislikes the call center job and wishes to be more worthy of something useful than helping out foreigners with problems that a person with an average IQ can figure out himself.

Today's youth are more interested in the American style of living as they work in US-style environments and speak to Americans for hours each day. Young men working in call centers have a lot of girlfriends and often change them like Vroom changing them every three months. The young women ape the dressing style of the Americans. They wear sleeveless tops, jeans, and skirts. They also indulge in lot of drinking and partying. Present day youth are averse towards political leaders. Vroom thinks that politicians alone are responsible for making India a poor nation. 'That is the only damn reason. Because the losers who have run our country for the last fifty years couldn't do better than make India one of the poorest countries on earth. Great job, thank you, dear great fucking leaders'. (*One night @ the call center*, 119)

The present generations of youngsters are more influenced by the use of Internet. They gather a lot of information from the various websites. Vroom gets all the information about bikes, jobs, politics, dating tips etc. only from the net. Internet also has certain negative influence on young people. Bakshi is found to have both the positive and negative influences of surfing the internet. When Vroom checks for the websites visited by Bakshi in his system, he finds, "Times of India.com, rediff.com,' etc. He also finds some more.'There is more. Aha, here is what I was looking for: awesomeindia.com–the best porn site for Indian girls, adultfriendfinder.com–a sex personals site, cabaretlounge.com–a strip club in Boston, porn-inspector.com...hello, the list goes on in this department.'(one *night @ the call center*, 175)This is a clear picture of what the youth of today confronted with culture.

Due to the fast speed technological developments nowadays, every call center employee needs to upgrade his technical skills which Bakshi often demands from Shyam, but wastes no opportunity not to allow him to become skillful.

Due to stress, many of them smoke too much and many quit the industry. In the novel *One Night @ the Call Center*Shyam and Vroom are found smoking often during their leisure time as well as the working hours due to stress. Working night shift they lose sleep and on top of this they have attempted irritated and angry customers. As a result, the employees face high stress levels on the daily basis. Many a time the customers do not respect the employees. They are rude to them and these people in the call center have no option but to accept it.To overcome their stress these people indulge in drinking, visit dance floors, listen to loud jarring music and involve in drunken fights and partying. To them 'A fight means a party is totally rocking.' This constant and continuing stress frustrates Vroom.

'Every night I come here and let people fuck me,' Vroom said and picked up the telephone headset. 'The Americans fuck me with this, in my ears hundreds of times a night. Bakshi fucks me with his management theories, backstabbing and threats to fire us. And the funny thing is, I let them do it. For money, for security—I let it happen. Come fuck me some more (one *night @ the call center*, 184)

Unable to overcome their stress many of them smoke too much and many quit the industry. Apart from this stress, young people working in call centers lose their identity in the society. They are called by American names, and they speak in the American accent.

Even their sport attitudes are like that of their peers in New York or other American cities. In the novel ShyamMehra is known as Sam Marcy, RadhikaJha as Regina Jones, Esha Singh as Eliza Singer and Varun Malhotra as Victor Mell. Their names are usually changed as the American tongues have trouble pronouncing their real names.

Present day young women are more concerned about their appearance and dressing. They restrict themselves to eat very less like Esha, even when the dish tastes too good. Priyanka is also more concerned about it. When she goes out with her boy friendShyam to restaurants, she is very choosy about the food she eats. These girls like "Esha hardly eat anything, but still jump around asking for treats(one *night @ the call center*,, 61) When Priyanka offered sweets to her friends for being proposed by Ganesh, 'Radhika took two pieces, while Esha broke the tiniest piece possible with human fingers. I guess the low-cut jeans figure comes at a price.' (One *night @ the call center*,, 60)

These girls are also more concerned about their dressing. They prefer wearing ornaments that matches the colour of their dress. Priyanka is not willing to wear even gold necklace that her mother forces to wear. She feels it would not fit her dress. She wore a blue tie-and-dye skirt, and a T-shirt that had a peace sign on it. It was typical Priyanka stuff. She wore earrings with blue beads, which matched her necklace... 'Why don't you wear the gold necklace I gave for your last birthday?'... 'no mom, it won't go with my dress. Yellow metal is totally uncool, only aunties wear it,' (one *night @ the call center*,, 45)

Among all these struggles and frustrations, these youngsters suffer existential crisis. However, their crisis is resolved by a divine intervention in the novel i.e., a phone call from God. This God presented in the novel is cool and does not preach them but simply asks them to listen to their inner call. This call becomes a turning point in their lives.

They regain their confidence, work out a master plan and finally succeed in saving their jobs in Connexions. These young people are talented enough to pursue their own dreams and contribute to the nation and the society. But in this pressing situation, they forget about those dreams. Only their inner voice can revive those dreams.

Chetan has tried to portray the world of call centers that has become a symbol of India's newly globalised economy. Through this novel, he communicates the experiences of the growing Indian middle class youth. The Indian BPO industry must realize that to keep growing, it must not only keep its customers but also its employees happy. Majority of the country men only read about BPOs, and call centers. They have had no idea of the people working there and the dilemmas they face. Bhagat's novel has served well in this need by depicting the trials and tribulations of the youth working at the call centers.(Ambigavathi-2010)

Cross culture encounter

The world is being viewed as a global village with all its Cultural, Social and Political differences, disappearing and walls of multiplicity and an indifferent, unconnected distant behaviour in trouble and enabling the world to emerge as a unified and cultural whole.

The cultural background of the societies of many 'Third World' regions are in full stagnation despite political and economic changes, traditional societies, following settled ways of living that have existed for hundreds, even thousands of years . In fact, to appreciate the ways in which firm moral standards operated in England during the eighteenth century to create great imaginative literature and art and to develop new forms of writing, but a step away from understanding the way similarly strong, established moral ideas express themselves in the literature of the 'Third World'. Literature of quality may even prove a more reliable bridge to other cultures then the words of politicians, since a good writer will consciously and unconsciously reflect the ideas that are currently shaping culture background.(Yasmine Goonerate1980)

The central theme about cross-cultural encounter ChetanBhagat's novel: **"2 states- the story of my marriage".** "Cross-cultural encounter are no mystery to the inhabitants of the Indian subcontinent. It is an ever-present reality. ChetanBhagat's**"2 states *-the story of my marriage*"** deals with this issue. Partly autobiographical, the tale of two people belonging to two different states and communities is weaved together with instances from the author's own life. Their relationship traverses the stages of friendship, passion and love to the decision to get married, but they have to overcome the ultimate test, staunch opposition to their union from their respective parents, whether their love proves strong enough to win over their families. The reluctance of people of different states to bridge cultural difference especially when it is an inter caste; inter community or interstate marriage in India. The author has excellently converted this accepted unfair reality into a perfect and full-fledged story and the author's slightly wicked sense of humours fundamental the narrative at various places serves to show real-life situations with genuineness and naturalness.

Chetan Bhagat has hailed as the most popular, important and biggest selling Indian author in English Language. India is well known for its varied cultural heritage as it is known for the lively and traditionally diverse marriages. '2 States' is a story of a marriage that is as simple as it can get, yet so complicated. ChetanBhargat's novel concentrates on how a particular phenomenon, the concept of love relates to matters to ideology, race, social class and gender. It also concentrates in terms of social, political and economic situation. The novel 2 states deals with the cross-cultural encounter complimenting the different experiences and imbibing them meaningfully. As a rose symbolizes beauty, as a soldier symbolizes nation, the title of any work should symbolizes the theme. Chetanbhagat's 2 states-the title by itself showcases the association point of the two states coming into union. A simple but realistic novel, brilliantly explores the encounter of two states; Punjab and Tamilnadu. The two main characters cut their umbilical cord to be affixed with a new cord; the marital cord. With the merger of two souls in the name of love, there is a blending of two cultures, religions, languages, tradition and practices. Thus, the two major characters shed their umbilical cord- their affectionate identity-and require a new identity.

Out of the several methods of marriage, two are predominant namely love marriage and arranged marriage. The boy and girl lead to love marriage and generally and simply they take this decision. In the current scenario, the instances of love marriage are increasing, but these differ from country to country. But multiplicity of languages, castes and community in India, this situation is small different. The girl's family should love the boy and the boy's family should love the girl If in the meantime, the love between the girl and the boy continues, they get married with the blessings of the two families and live happily thereafter. In India, arranged marriages are more common. In a situation of love between two persons that too from different district, languages or communities and their parents and families, do not generally agree. A number of cause, the lovers' rebel, elope; perform court marriage without the permission/ presence of their parents or do suicide A best method is to try to convince the two family members, even if it obtain some time. (This novel by ChetanBhagat is said to be the real story of his own marriage, although many names etc.)

This novel revolves around **Krish**and **Ananya;** hailing from two different states in India and their simple love story laced with details as they decide to take the thrust. The families do not approve of the various traditions and think low of the future of their marital harmony. This novel is a take on inter-religious marriages and their assumed ambiguity in India. '2 States' by ChetanBhagat takes you on a splendid journey to the land of mystic majesty India. Boy from Punjab fall in love with a girl from Tamil Nadu and they decide to tie the knot. This novel is concerning an IIMA couple's struggle to marry over the cultural differences. Krish is north Indian Punjabi boy in love with Tamilian Brahmin girl Ananya. The only catch is, Krish and Ananya don't want to elope or be estranged to their families, and therefore, they choose to convince their parents for the marriage.

Both Ananya and Krish take turns to win over each other's families like each other. In fact, Krish does get 4 gold rings made to purpose girl's entire family! Though the idea is most realistic, it draws ones attention to cultural differences in various India. In India cross-cultural marriages are still looked upon critically let alone an inter-state marriage. Added to that Punjabis are clearly different from Tamilians; Punjabis are well known for their disorder, richness and easy attitude while Tamilians for their good manners and uncommunicativeness. However, the couple in question is exceptions and very much in love. They prefer the difficult pathway of winning to the hearts of their parents and seek their blessings instead of eloping.

Bhagat manages to provide an interesting perspective to a common problem faced by teenagers today, family opponent when they get married out of community and inter-state. "Culture modifies for definite, but the move in people's thoughts, viewpoint and globe view is usual. Culture is not just our food, arts and traditions in a broader sense, culture defines it, who are as people, how aim to live their lives, what acceptable or unacceptable behaviour and who in society is rewarded and punished. Most important, our culture contains the implicit rules by which we live – our values"Bhagat has a more difficult time describing values within Indian culture" When think of Indian values, we normally think of personal values – such as family, religion and respect for elders and it is notable in Indian. The intention of the novel is good. It wants to bring out the racial prejudices that still exist among people belonging to different states and more evident as North-South divide.

There are two ways to look at the racial comments and humour in this novel. Punjabi characters making racial comments about South Indians, may be this what happened in his real life and author wanted to be true to the characters Even Krish making some observations about Tamil culture and habits is bit understandable: Punjabi boy landing in Chennai for first time and getting bothered with new people around him.

The novel is first in its content that attempts to unite not only two states but also their traditions and cultures. It endeavors to represent the people of the nation only as Indians not as castes, religious, states etc. This is the only thing the novelist wants to carry to the youth of his country. With Krish and Ananya hailing from two different regions, matters only take to worse. This novel delicately puts across these obvious differences in mindsets. The mismatch in the mental frameworks is absolutely, the way he brings in the differences and takes potshots at each other's cultural differences is bone tickling. Though the basis is most realistic, it draws your attention to cultural differences in diverse India. (Jai Arjun Singh-2009)

Bhagat manages to provide an interesting perspective to a common problem faced by youngsters today, family opposition when marrying out of community and interstate of different states to bridge cultural differences. ChetanBhagat highly appealing and tell the originality of the Indian society and its culture and tradition which is far more different from the western lifestyle and Marriage system. ChetanBhagat novels several have objected to the relations an either too simplistic or perpetuating patriarchal value and ChetanBhagat truly captures the essence of different India culture.

Conclusion

He is dealing with the harsh realities of life and modern culture life of young generation and problem faced by the young generation in his works etc. He brings about corporate culture is a term used to describe beliefs and a value system that provides its unique taste and attitude to a friendship in Cosmo-culture the condition of youth is very pathetic. In this world of Cosmo-culture, everybody is involved in an extra marital relationship. He selects subject which he reader can associate with modern culture. He has faction with a mix of sentiment, romance, religion relationship, culture ,economic and family relationship and also social message depicted in ChetanBhagat novels several have objected to the relations an either too simplistic or perpetuating patriarchal value and also he truly captures the essence of modern India culture. ChetanBhagat had a great role in bringing those Indian readers back to books. Though he has a high commercial purpose in his novels, his main intention was to consider the readers. Bhagat's success is that he addresses the everyday concerns of India's middle-class youth, in a language they can relate to, and also consciously strives for a mass appeal.

References

1. Bhagatchetan. '**Five Point someone**' published by Rupa.co, New Delhi, 2004.
2. Bhagatchetan. '**One Night @the call center**' published by Rupa.co, NewDelhi, 2005.
3. Bhagatchetan. '**The 3 mistakes of my life**' published by Rupa.co, Newdelhi, 2008.
4. Bhagatchetan. '**2 states-the story of my marriage**' published by Rupa.co, Newdelhi, 2009.
5. Ajgaonkar-Nayak, Smitha. **The Youth in Three Mistakes of My Life.** Cyber Literature 21.2 (Dec 2008): 101-105.
6. 2. MalshetteYogeshTrimbakrao. **"A Critique Study of ChetanBhagat's '2 States: The Story of My Marriage' in Indian Context".** An International Journal in English, Vol-I, Issue-X, July 2012.
7. ShitalbabuA.Tayade,Ramkrushna Mahavidyalaya, Darapur, Amravati. **"Social Reflection in ChetanBhagat's Novels,"** Contemporary Research in India.Vol: 1, Issue: III, Spetember, 2011.
8. Hemalatha.K, "**ChetanBhagat and AravindAdiga**: New voices of New India." The Vedic Path 83.3 and 4 (July-Dec 2009): 21-23
9. Fredeicks,S.C.: "**Lucian's True History as SF**", Science Fiction Studies, Vol.55, No. 1(March 1976). pp.49-60
10. Georgiadou, Aristoula&Larmour, David H.J.: "**Lucian's Science Fiction Novel True Histories. Interpretation and Commentary**", Mnemosyne Supplement 179. Leiden 1998.
11. Clute, John and Peter Nicholls, eds., "**The Encyclopedia of Science Fiction**". St Albans, Herts, UK: Granada Publishing, 1979.
12. Wolfe, Gary K. "**Critical Terms for Science Fiction and Fantasy**: A Glossary and Guide to Scholarship", New York: Greenwood Press, 1986.

13. Bhagat, Chetan. "**One Night at the CallCenter**". Published by Rupa& co, New Delhi, 2005.
14. Hemalatha.K, "**ChetanBhagat and AravindAdiga**: New voices of New India." The Vedic Path 83.3 and 4 (July-Dec 2009): 21-23.
15. Liam Connell. "**E-terror: Computer viruses, Class and Tranationalism in Transmission and One Night @ the CallCenter**". Journal of Postcolonial Writing, Vol.46, Nos.3-4, July/September 2010, 279-290.
16. . Singh, Jai Arjun. "**The End of Presentation.**" Biblio: a review of books 14.3 and 4 (Mar-Apr 2009).
17. J.A. Cuddon. **The Penguin Dictionary of literary Terms and Literary theory**. Penguin Books.
18. Ms.NiyatiB.Bhatt. ChetanBhagat's **one night @ the call center** as a Popular Fiction. Nations Vol.II No.1.
19. Ashcroft, Bill Gareth Griffiths and Helen Tiffin, eds. **The Post Colonial Studies Reader**. 1995. Rpt. London: Routledge, 1997.
20. Fanon, Frantz, **Black Skin. White Masks.** Trans. Charles Lam Markmann. New York: Groves Press, 1967.
21. Jakhar, Sunita. ChetanBhagat's**The Three Mistakes of My Life**: A Post Colonial Reading, 2010.
22. .Ankitapatel. **"Youth Sensibility and Spiritualism in One Night@ the Call Center"**.International online e-journal, vol-II,issue-3,February 2010.
23. 6.Prasun Banerjee. **"The Choreographed Narrative: Recontextualising the Narrative Strategies in ChetanBhagat's Fiction** "An International Journal in English ,Vol-III,Issue-I,March 2012.
24. 7.R,A.Vats and Rakhi Sharma.**"ChetanBhagat: A Libertarian"**. An International Journal in English,Vol-II,Issue-II,June 2011.
25. 8.JadhavArvindTukaram. **"Representing Metropolitan Youth Culture: An assessment of ChetanBhagat's Five Point someone and One Night @ the Call Center".** An International journal in English Vol-III, Issue-II, 5th June2012.
26. https://shodhganga.inflibnet.ac.in/bitstream/10603/96676/7/

07_chapter1.pdf

27. https://en.wikipedia.org/wiki/Indian_English_literature
28. 8hagat, Chctan. *What Yollng India Wants.* Ncw Delhi: Rupa Publications India, 2012. Print.
29. Mukherjee, Meenakshi. *Realism Ami Reality: The Novel And Society In India.* Oxford University Press, 1985. Print.
30. Narayan, Shyamala; Jon Mee. "Novelists Of 1950s And 19605." Mehrotra, A.K. *An*
31. *Li/Ustrated 1fistory Of Indian Litera/Lire In English.* Orient 8lackswan, 2003. 230.Print.
32. R.Parthasarthy, "Tradition And Creativity: Stylistic Innovations In Raja Rao" Larry Smith(Ed.)Discourse *Across Cultllre: Strategics In World English* London Prentice
33. Rao, Raja. *Kan/Ilapura.* Ncw Delhi: Oxford University Press, 2010. Print.
34. Tagore, Rabindranath. *Crisis In Civilization &Other Essays.* Rupa, 2003. Print.
35. Williams, H.M, *Indo-Anglian Literature ISOO-J970:A Survey,* New Delhi: Orient Longman. 1976,

Printed by Libri Plureos GmbH in Hamburg, Germany